FIVE GATES

THE SCIENCE OF HEALING
THE SPIRIT

By The Same Author

RECOVER WITH ME

A Classic Recovery Manual Which Brings the
12-Step Program Into the 21st Century

FREE TO LOVE MY LIFE

Audio Tape Series to Help Us Take Ourselves
Through the Five Gates Program

KNOW MYSELF = HELP MYSELF

Audio Tape Series and Workbook for Troubled
Teenagers

THE JOYFUL RECOVERY SHOW

A Television Series Dedicated Primarily to the
Family Members of Addicted and Suffering
People

FIVE GATES

THE SCIENCE OF HEALING THE SPIRIT

Accelerated Deep Emotional Healing

LYNN N. KESSELMAN
PSYCHOTHERAPIST, CCDC

RECOVERY PRESS, INC.

For information, contact Recovery Press, Inc. at

Publisher@FiveGates.com

(888) 551-4243

Library of Congress Control Number: 2004117856

Published by Recovery Press, Inc.

Cover Design by Kim G. McNally

www.FiveGates.com

Notice: The Five Gates Training Program has a pending patent which prohibits its commercial use by any practitioner or institution without the written permission of Recovery Management Service Co. Inc. The developer of the Five Gates has granted permission that all who wish to take themselves through the Five Gates Program are welcome to do so.

Printed in the United States of America.

FIRST EDITION, 2004

ACKNOWLEDGEMENTS

This book was the result of my work with more than three hundred Five Gates clients, and my observations from a great many more people I met in recovery fellowships. Additionally, most noteworthy of the individual contributors to my work and this book are:

Editing and Support

Kim G. McNally, Chief Editorial Advisor and Coordinator, whose inspired suggestions were invaluable.

Ira Victor, my wise friend, who helped me see the best parts of this book.

Lynn Casella for her professional editing talents and delightful spirit.

Allison Mead, professional editor.

Jokichi "Joe" Takamine, M.D., Cert. Addiction Medicine, whose faith in my work helped it to become visible.

Max Schneider, M.D., Cert. Addiction Medicine, who saw the uniqueness of my ideas and encouraged me to bring them to the medical community.

John Drimmer, Ph.D., Psychology, who supported so many of my ideas early in the writing of this book.

Jerry Schoenkopf who published an overview summary of The Five Gates in the Heroin Times.

The hundreds of men who shared their personal histories and ideas at New Hope Village, our former half-way house in Florida.

Rabbi Mortachi Gafni who was my first teacher of Torah/ Talmud.

Donald Margolis who introduced me to the wisdom of the Kabbalah, and whose generosity made possible much of my work with indigent clients.

Habib Davanloo, M.D., whose work in the brief time-limited psychotherapy, though different from my own, confirmed my earliest beliefs in the irreversibility of neurological, chemical damage. His work also confirmed my belief that clients could get well very quickly, and more easily than if they had done so slowly.

The American Psychiatric Association, which through their many graduate courses and seminars, gave me an understanding of the contours of the present knowledge of the Mental Health Professions.

Special Acknowledgments

Corrine Shukartsi whose encouragement and support made the publication of this book possible.

Sadie Kesselman, my mother, who didn't like much of what I had to say, but encouraged me nonetheless.

Louis Kesselman (deceased), my father, who from my earliest childhood encouraged the scientist and humanitarian in me

Thomas Breen - When I was suffering, he brought me love. When my suffering past, he brought me wisdom. When I craved to share, he taught me how. Without him, the darkness would have consumed too many of us.

And last but not least, all of my clients, whose trust made my work possible. Their remarkable recoveries made me know that this program is important to all of us.

FORWARD BY
RABBI ABRAHAM J. TWERSKI, M.D.

In *Recover With Me,* Lynn Kesselman describes how his program for recovery, patterned after the 12-steps of Alcohol Anonymous, can enable a person to integrate the 12-steps rather than just comply with them. This is achieved by a thorough understanding and clarification of the steps.

Not being satisfied with even the triumph of overcoming addiction, Kesselman goes on, in *Five Gates — The Science of Healing the Spirit,* to show how a person can achieve emotional healing via fulfilling the needs of the human spirit.

Over and above contributing to recovery from alcohol or other chemical dependency, *Five Gates* can also be of great help to people who have no substance abuse problem, or for that matter, any other addiction. Anxiety, fear, depression, disillusionment, and relationship problems are not unique to alcoholics, chemically dependent people, or other addicts. These are problems of the human condition, and ironically, may have increased in incidence as science, technology and medicine have made life more comfortable.

The marvelous advances in the sciences have addressed the physical needs of man, focusing on the "how" of life. The "why" of life is not in their realm. Yet, the physical component of man is not the whole of man. The uniqueness of man lies in the human spirit. All the comforts and conveniences that science and technology can provide do not provide the universally sought-after happiness. Man can be happy only when his spiritual as well as physical needs are satisfied.

Five Gates provides a methodology whereby a person can become whole. The gates of Five Gates are gates to happiness.

Dr. Twerski is certified in psychiatry and is one of the best known clinicians, authors, and philosophers in spirituality and the addictions field with more than seventy books to his credit.

FORWARD BY
MAX A. SCHNEIDER, M.D., FASAM

It has been said that, "There are many roads to Rome." Lynn Kesselman has paved another in his *Five Gates — The Science of Healing The Spirit*. Attacking the full spectrum of the psycho/social/spiritual/physical disease of addiction, *Five Gates* beautifully recognizes the interrelation of these four components and that wellness (which is also called sobriety) demands a fine tuned balance of all four components. Kesselman draws attention to the mind, body and spirit evolving in an intriguing and methodical manner. Altering our thoughts, emotions and spirituality also alters our physiology and medical health. Uniquely defining spirituality, *Five Gates* directs you to a clearer understanding of just what this very necessary life component is about — thus enabling your light of awareness to turn on and clarity to emerge.

Addiction is a chronic, not an acute illness. It is a progressive disease. It demands our continuing attention. These Gates might well be traversed over and over. Gate by Gate one progresses from illness, confusion and fear to clarity and hopefulness; from poor health to wellness; from slavery to freedom. Such a road can bring joy to all, especially the addicted.

My first impression was that *Five Gates* is a post-graduate course to the original "12 Steps." I still think this is true. I also believe that the *Five Gates* process might be called "autopsychoanalysis." Yes, it can be done solo but, like author Kesselman, I believe that for the most powerful results the use of an instructor is wisest.

The *Five Gates* is a call for action and is not instead of Alcoholics Anonymous (or any of AA's offshoots such as Narcotics Anonymous, Nicotine Anonymous, etc.) but in addition to these important life saving programs.

Max Schneider, M.D.'s credentials are on the reverse page.

Max Schneider, M.D. is a Fellow and past president of the American Society of Addiction Medicine (ASAM), the Past Chair of the Board of Directors of the National Council on Alcoholism and Drug Dependence (NCADD), is a Clinical Professor of Psychiatry (Addiction Medicine) at the University of California at Irvine College of Medicine, and was past president of the California Society of Addiction Medicine.

FORWARD BY
MR. ROY EVANS

I have served as President and Executive Director for Bridge Back Correctional Re-Entry Facility (prison) for the past 35 years where I have attended to the needs of countless recovering people. I have come to see recovery from addictions as only one dimension of a far greater need. The greater need touches all of us; we need a firm connection with a sense of faith that we can have a good life free from anxiety, depression, addictions and all of the emotional and mental disorders which typically plague almost every inmate at Bridge Back.

The early vision for Bridgeback was that we would help our inmates recover from substance addictions, but early on we learned that all who suffer from this affliction also suffer from anxieties, depression, and other emotional and mental disorders. They are connected in ways brilliantly and thoroughly explained in *Five Gates — The Science of Healing the Spirit*. We've all dreamed that one day there would be a magic pill that would banish these problems, but until now it seemed as though such a universal answer would be many years in coming.

Five Gates — The Science of Healing the Spirit is not a pill but it is the first program I have seen which holds the promise of arresting and reversing the epidemic which keeps mine and all other prisons full and the courts overwhelmed with an endless supply of new disturbed and addicted offenders. *Five Gates* starts by helping us see how we have become who we are and continues to describe not only how we would ideally be, but also gives us a method by which we can improve ourselves quickly.

At first it seemed wrong to believe that one program could solve all of these problems at the same time and quickly. We have fellowships for alcoholism, narcotic addictions, cocaine addictions, rage disorder, eating disorders, sexual compulsions, emotional unrest, and countless others. We have medical specialists for every one of these, yet so few people really get well. I believe that Lynn Kesselman has hit on the method for tying all of these together into a single perspective and treatment method for reversing their underlying cause, the dysfunctional fears which drive people into these states of disrepair. The Five Gates Program attacks these problems at their root which we all knew was anchored in us from our childhood. Now we have a tool, independent from expensive and long drawn out medical treatments, to cleanse our selves from these early in life dysfunctional beliefs. The fact that it does this so quickly comes less surprising as we visit with Lynn personally on the pages of this book and discover for the first time we have found a tool for seeing and repairing the original problem.

For those who have believed that they could not understand a presentation or method of sweeping importance, this book will soon change their mind. Lynn has a way of expressing the truth in terms we can all understand.

AUTHOR'S FORWORD

A statement I've heard at A.A. and elsewhere has always touched me, "You are not alone." I have drawn heavily from my own life in the hope that you receive some value from my experience. I have had many clients whose lives seemed very similar in some ways to my own. Before our spiritual awakening, it's hard for us to see how much we are all alike. Although, at the beginning of my own recovery the stories of others who have walked this path successfully gave me hope and helped me feel much less alone.

For many years, I wandered through life trying vocations and relationships one after another. It seemed on the surface that I was often successful at first, but then I always did something that was self-defeating, something that forced me to move on to something new. I didn't consciously realize this, but I was searching for something that would give me the feeling that I'd finally proven I was worthy of love. Then I wouldn't have to be and feel so alone. But even when it seemed to be going well, I still felt so empty and alone. Most of my clients have experienced these same feelings, and tell stories much like mine.

When I felt the anxieties of being alone and unloved, I drank alcohol to numb my pain and lessen my fears. For the first fifty-five years of my adult life, I seriously doubt I could have spent one year, and possibly not even a month without drinking, though there were years, my happiest years, in which I did not heavily abuse alcohol.

Starting in my mid-forties, the shoes of my life became unbearably tight, and I aggressively self-medicated my anxieties with more and more alcohol. By the time I was fifty-three, and for the following two years, I lived very few hours sober. I slept so poorly that I became haggard, wasted and worn. I hid from people who had known me when I had been able to put up a better front.

I drank so much every day that it felt normal, and being sober felt abnormal. I woke up every morning with a need for a drink. That drink was usually a pint of vodka before I could feel "normal" again. I was trapped in my own self-destructive cycle and didn't know why, or how to escape falling further into ruin of every kind. But I knew it wasn't alcohol that was my jailer, it was my mind.

Mine is the story of an alcoholic. But despite the ruinous effects of my drinking, the real lesson for me has little to do with alcohol. I stopped on July 15th of 1995, not only because of alcohol, but because I was so despondent and empty. The alcohol didn't work anymore. I thought there was no reason for me to live another day of misery. I put a gun in my mouth and only by the miracle of my momentarily coming to my senses was I able to reluctantly remove it and call for help.

Thank God for the help of other sufferers who had gained better lives from their near ruin. With no spiritual direction, no purpose to my life, no real source of satisfaction or identity, with their help and support I managed to go four months without a drink. If not for the miracle of my spiritual awakening that came to me next, I doubt there would have been a fifth month. In what seemed like a single moment in time, it all came together for me. I suddenly saw that something in me was causing my real problems and I could fix them by fixing me! Everyone else probably knew this but for years I kept struggling to try to fix the world outside of me. It was my fear of drinking and the fact that I couldn't deny that my life could not go on as it was, that gave me my first commitment to stop drinking. But this didn't solve my real problem.

During my first sober months I was still so unhappy deep inside that I felt it wouldn't have made much difference whether I drank or not. Relief finally came when I could clearly see that I could change in ways that would give me a better life. Back then that's all I knew. Eventually my realizations about what was driving my own suffering, and later my growing wellness, made it possible for me not only to help myself but later to help other struggling sufferers, both sober and not. My well of despair and how I rose from it to have a happy life is what has given me a loving hand to reach out to you. The Five Gates, which resulted from my quest for wellness, is your program, if you'll take it.

Dedication To Seekers of Truth & My Suffering Brothers and Sisters

Suffering is not only pain; it is the hopeless feeling that our pains have no solution. It makes us feel alone because we are convinced no one really knows or cares about how we feel.

If you think no one cares about how you feel, you may be right, even though people may also tell you they care about you and want to help you. Too often they don't know that how you feel is your real problem. The main thing that matters is how you feel about yourself. As your love for being who you are increases, you will feel less alone. In wellness, our worries about ourselves diminish and we are able to positively experience our connections with everything and everyone. As you feel more connected to life your feelings of being alone will quickly leave you.

Do you believe recovery or getting well is accomplished by stopping "using" or not doing things others, or even you don't want you to do? It's not. Instead, it's learning how to be happy, which means training ourselves to banish needless fears. When you are happy, you can most easily achieve the changes in yourself, which will change your world. Working the Five Gates Program here will positively change your reality.

A lot of the problems we see in our selves are caused by "using." Using is not only our misadventures with drugs or other negative habits, it's a much larger idea about how we run away from life into habitual patterns which we use to keep ourselves from seeing life on terms we find uncomfortable. Using is a method by which we misdirect our minds and senses to help us cope with our self-doubts and fears. Drugs, gambling, obsessive thoughts and compulsive, escapist actions are just a small part of that list. Recovery is equivalent to feeling great and no longer feeling the need to escape reality at all. It's not about your willpower or fighting your destructive thoughts and actions, it's about losing your interest in thinking about, believing in, and doing those destructive things to which you are addicted. When you're well, life becomes easier, and not so much of a battle. If you can start caring more about yourself, and caring less about how others feel about you, you'll be well on the road to recovery immediately. The only other things you'll need are a belief you can give yourself a happier, and a more secure life. You will need some special thinking tools for navigating life as a more powerful person, and practice. That's what you will find here.

How can you accomplish these things? First, you must accept that although the world has seemed uncooperative with your needs, and you're probably right about that, the only problems you can and need to fix are inside you. If this seems wrong to you, don't be surprised. One of our most destructive symptoms of our lack of confidence in our own abilities to solve our problems is our need to put the blame outside ourselves. That's because when we don't know how to fix ourselves, we believe blaming ourselves would just make us feel worse. But there is no need for blame at all since all we want to do is empower ourselves.

Second, you'll need to work hard in the Fourth and Fifth Gates of the Five Gates Training Program, which are the ones that clear the now deeply-implanted beliefs about yourself, which started your low self-esteem problems, usually in your childhood. Later in this book, you'll see several explanations of how and why this process works and how to do it. When you clear the negative psychological effects of your childhood to the degree necessary, all you need to do is study and learn some common sense life navigation principles.

Last, and for as long as it takes, you can make these new insights and principles an integral part of who you are, by your practice applying them in all of your daily activities and thoughts. That's it!!

The first and most intensive part of this program is called the Five Gates Core Training. Following the Core Training, and throughout our lives, we keep ourselves well and improve by daily maintenance, the Life Practice. More than 95% of my clients have experienced a "spiritual awakening" in less than a week of going through the Core Training, and 80% have stuck to the Five Gates Life Practice methods well enough to turn their perceptions, feelings and lives around, often to such a great degree that not only they, but everyone else can feel the positive change in them immediately. You can do this too, if you're willing to open your mind and try your best to master the Five Gates Training Program for yourself.

Good luck,
Lynn N. Kesselman
Five Gates Founder & Developer

GOALS OF THIS BOOK

If this book does its job as I have intended, it will serve the needs of sufferers, seekers, discontents, healers and teachers. Family members and friends of sufferers will discover here a much better insight into emotional mental health problems and there solutions. The Five Gates Training Program is a philosophy, as well as an operational healing and guidance program. With it we can see and reconcile the root causes of our emotional problems that have driven us to our anxieties, depressions and addictions of all kinds. We can also cleanse ourselves of the disabling ideas that came upon us from these root causes and train ourselves to process reality in a new way that gives us happiness, personal empowerment and much more productive lives. The Five Gates is a way of living.

The Table of Contents is a suggestive flow of topics covered in the mainstream of this book's presentation. Some of the topics are touched upon and even presented in more than one place in the book. This is necessary to provide continuity and a more holistic understanding of what I experience as a single, integrated whole, rather than a collection of fragmented facts and methods.

If at times you feel as though you are finding yourself on these pages, then one of my greatest goals for this book will have been achieved. We can only learn from what we accept as real, and we can only accept as real that which is rooted in and connects us to our own experiences.

How To Navigate This Book

My Five Gates Training client's receive much less philosophical background than you will find in this book, prior to my taking them through the Fourth and Fifth Gates. This approach works fine because in a face-to-face environment I can learn a good deal about their backgrounds and can pick just those insights necessary to prepare them for their spiritual awakening, which is the key ingredient to opening our minds to the mental awakening we need to help us manage our lives efficiently and pleasurably in present time.

Some clients need considerable encouragement and support before they can effectively apply themselves to completing the detailed life survey questionnaire, which is the Fourth Gate and the basis for their becoming ready for the journey through the Fifth Gate. Here I have attempted to provide a clear understanding of the basis of this program before we attempt to navigate the process of healing our inner child from the fear producing effects of our childhood misconceptions about ourselves and life.

Some people will question whether or not the problems they experienced later in life were actually the result of childhood experiences and misperceptions. Even if later life experiences seem to trigger their present difficulties, they will discover as they journey through the Five Gates that early life always sets us up for our inability to process these later stresses. This is why some people can experience grave losses or setbacks much better than others.

As you begin to read the philosophical sections you will find much that you already know. Patiently examine each idea and proceed as quickly as you are satisfied that you understand it, even though there will be many that you will understand that you have not yet been able to consistently put to use in your daily life. Consider this section to be a method of preparing yourself for your Fourth and Fifth Gates' healing journey.

Although you may want to go quickly through the philosophical section you will be most benefited by taking each of the Five Gates with painstaking thoroughness since they build a healing sequence which is at the heart of the Five Gates training itself.

Our Fourth and Fifth Gates heal us from the disabling effects of the beliefs we mistakenly accepted about ourselves and life as children. The philosophy section, which is mirrored more tangibly in the Second and Third Gates gives us a road map for how to continue the healing of our spirits and make the most of life in the present. When you have completed your Fifth Gate journey you will be ready to re-travel through the philosophical section with much greater openness and understanding.

In this special method of training yourself to be your own psychotherapist, I encourage you to be very attuned to your own intuition as you make your way through this book. You may be reading this book for the purpose of adding to your general insights about yourself and life without any intention of taking yourself through the Five Gates process. In this case, the Table of Contents will provide a useful navigational guide to those areas which interest you most. If you are a mental health professional please keep in mind that the Five Gates process carries a pending patent prohibiting anyone from taking others through this program for commercial or using its name in connection with your work without the permission of Recovery Management Service which governs the licensed use of the Five Gates Program, the title of "Certified Five Gates Trainer" or the use of the Five Gates name in describing your work without certification. More information is available at www.fivegates.com.

TABLE OF CONTENTS

PART FIVE

PART SIX - APPENDICES

PART ONE

THE FIVE GATES PHILOSOPHY

_____

How Do I Know If I Need Recovery? From What?

"Am I happy?" It seems clear that if you are happy you are not going to want to change anything about yourself. The key to seeing if you are happy is to ask yourself the followings questions. "How completely do I enjoy being who I am right now?" "Do I say or do self-destructive things?" "Do I feel anxiety much of the time, even when I am faced with no important losses?" "Do I have problems getting myself to do things that my judgment tells me I should be doing?" "Do I feel lonely and isolated, but can't get myself to take any steps to connect with other people?" "Am I ashamed of being who I am?" "Do I have problems obeying the law?" "Do I abuse alcohol, other drugs, sex, gambling, food, or any other addictive behavior?" "Do I find myself unable to accept and let go of past disappointments?" "Do you experience anger, resentments or rage when you can see they do you more harm than good?" "Have I been diagnosed with any emotional or mental disorders?" "Do I tend to alienate people around me or leave them with a poor impression of who I am?" "Am I frustrated about my inability to help myself? "

If you have any of these kinds of problems don't feel discouraged about them because you can greatly improve these problems and often can free yourself from them entirely by taking the Five Gates Training Program as it is found here. Don't believe anyone who says you can't.

We Need A New Way to See Ourselves and Life

If we find that we are unable to be unhappy, we need to change how we see ourselves. How can we do this? In place of our early life's learned judgments, what we all need is a more healing, accurate and positive way of seeing our worlds and ourselves. This is not a self-deceiving, feel-good way to accept our failures, but a better way to support our successes. We need to learn to place less faith in the importance of events and opinions outside ourselves and our control, and simply take comfort in the fact that we have only one responsibility, one ability and, therefore, only one job in life, to manage ourselves to our best abilities now. We must learn to accept our limitations without fear realizing they are not our shortcomings. We know we can't change the past, and cannot know the future until it becomes the present. This is why we must stop deceiving and torturing ourselves with negative beliefs and feelings. Our refusal to do this will cause us suffering because it takes us out of the present. We need to accept that our best efforts to feel connected to others, along with our capacities to enjoy pleasures, are the most important gifts we have in life.

A major benefit of working the Five Gates Training Program is that we free ourselves from disabling beliefs that tell us we have powers and responsibilities outside of the present. We free ourselves from the lie that we will gain power through negative attitudes or actions. Our learning to understand, accept, and use these truths is a major goal and benefit of the Five Gates Training Program. We become free to love others and ourselves without the need to judge anyone. The energy of our positive actions and thoughts are what heals us.

What is the Five Gates Program?

The Five Gates Program is more than a recovery program; it is a way of life. It gives us a new way of seeing ourselves, how we became who we are and how we can transform ourselves into the person we want to be. The Five Gates Program transforms us through sequenced thoughts and actions which are designed not so much to treat our symptoms, but to permanently heal us by removing the root causes of our anxieties, depressions, addictions and the destructive effects of our dysfunctional beliefs. It generates from within us a natural and lasting spiritual awakening based on easily understood logical truths, many of them taken from our personal life experience. It teaches us powerful living tools for navigating in the present. The Five Gates "Core Training" has two parts: the Mental Awakening (the first Three Gates) and the Spiritual Awakening (Gates Four and Five). Following the Fifth Gate, we begin "The Life Practice" which is our lifelong program of self-monitoring and improvement, which is even more empowering and pleasurable.

Most people who take the Five Gates Training Program have tried several other programs that didn't work. This does not indicate they have less chance of success in this program, often just the opposite. Most programs operate from the facilitator's perspective and do not intimately connect with the perspective of the person seeking help. Too often other programs put off the person needing help by being judgmental, illogical and superstitiously based. The Five Gates Program is a not only a powerful tool for correcting dysfunctional beliefs of those needing help, but it is a seamless, logical and powerfully intimate progression of healing truths and easily understood methods to cement and improve upon our progress. Most people who seek help in this area suffer from some degree of loss of focus. The Five Gates Program overcomes this problem by quickly cutting to the root of how we process reality. The speed at which we heal is not only convenient to our natural impatience, but also takes advantage of the fact that slow healing is more difficult in that it causes us to live in negative perspectives which provide no immediate relief.

Because the Five Gates Training positively transforms the way we process reality, it is a valuable tool for anyone who simply wants to feel better about him or herself and life. It often helps boost our intelligence by greatly improving our self-esteem and concentration abilities.

If you are not too severely emotionally troubled or impaired by your early life self-perceptions and the effects they've had on you later, you can take yourself through the Five Gates Training Program using this book as your instruction manual. As you travel along this healing journey, please read the book sequentially to make sure you have absorbed the ideas that can help you apply the program most effectively. If you can't work the Five Gates Training on your own or prefer to have a qualified facilitator take you through this program, we can find access to a certified trainer at our website, www.fivegates.com.

Why We Need the Five Gates Program

We all grew up, or later in life faced situations which to some degree left us with negative messages about ourselves and life. Examples of this are "you can't succeed," "you are not safe," "you do not deserve a good life," and "you are unlovable." These usually unconscious messages negatively influenced how our personalities developed and now haunt us, often without our even knowing it. These messages and our negative adjustments to the fears that they cause are our real prison and source of suffering. Through implementation of the program, we find and reject these messages to replace them with clear, positive perceptions, methods and actions. These truths will keep us feeling positive and performing to our best ability. Finally, we become able to finally live a relaxed and happy life. We lose our negative obsessions and compulsions. As we conclude the "Core Training," usually in less than a week, we learn tools, which reinforce our ability to rid ourselves of old messages and self-defeating thoughts and actions. When necessary, we reinforce our abilities to maintain our new, far more satisfying lives with Five Gates or other support groups. Quickly at first, then gradually to completion, we become the new happy and effective person we always wanted to be.

It is always important to remember that this process takes place inside of you, and therefore, if you use a facilitator, though this person may be very important, he or she is your guide, not your healer. Our pending patent forbids practitioners from using the Five Gates Training Program without proper licensing. But, since those taking the Program must be their own facilitator, it may be an advantage, especially if they are not too intellectually or emotionally disabled, and they are very motivated to seek out and embrace these healing changes for themselves.

The 80 plus percent success of the Five Gates Training Program is the measurement of our success with clients I have personally taken through this process. This Program is the same one I use in my practice. The only difference is that in taking yourself through this program, specifically your journey through the Fifth Gate, you will need to rely more heavily on yourself to draw the inferences from your life's history. We have included special aids to help you do this. If you follow the instructions and allow yourself to be carried along with the spirit of what is shared here, you will be healed.

The Five Gates Promises

- We become free of those addictions from which we desperately want to be freed. It changes how we feel so that we don't run away from our bad feelings through using.
- We learn more powerful insights about life and ourselves. These empower us and reduce our fears.
- We're finally free of our fears and resentments from our past, and never need to make new ones in our present or future.
- We become able to do and enjoy those things we wanted to do, but didn't know how to do before. Or perhaps we had trouble getting ourselves to do them when we were suffering.
- We forge new, positive relationships with new friends and casual acquaintances.
- We become able to express our thoughts and feelings. This helps us to regain positive family closeness and connections.
- We finally feel free, perhaps for the first time in our lives!

Will The Five Gates Program Stop Me from "Using"?

No! The Five Gates Training Program will end your cravings, and thereby support your decision to stop using.

Most people mistakenly believe that they are addicted because it still gives them pleasure. Actually, we use because we are compulsively trying to escape the anxiety we experienced before we took the Five Gates Training Program. At the conclusion of the Core Training portion of this program, we feel so well we have no cravings to use. But, we still must overcome our deeply ingrained lifestyle habits, which include using without thinking about it. Now, we can quit by adding our willpower to our spiritual awakening. The Five Gates Program gives us the power to do what we want to do about all of our lifestyle decisions. If we continue to use the tools we are taught in the Five Gates Training Program, we will feel spiritually wonderful and perform better in every aspect of our lives. Even our memory and intelligence are usually improved. People who take the Five Gates Program more easily trust this program because they see that we're not trying to control them, but instead are empowering them to feel whole.

Do I Need to Understand All of These Ideas For the Program to Work for Me?

Absolutely not. Every important idea of the Five Gates Training Program is repeated here often and stated in different ways. Even if you understood none of them, but simply followed the step-by-step instructions found in Part III, "It's Time to Begin Our Healing Journey," this program will still work for you. The purpose behind all of the explanations is to more thoroughly prepare you to navigate the Five Gates as quickly and as deeply as you can the first time you do it. You can always retake yourself through any of the Gates again and experience an even more complete healing. Most people take this journey only once because they feel an immediate relief and are more easily satisfied than I was. In my own "Life Practice" of the Five Gates Program, I find myself repeatedly going back over these ideas to help me avoid the occasional repetitions of my own wrong thinking about myself and new life situations.

Why Does the Five Gates Training Program Work So Fast?

We say that the Five Gates Training Program can change you in less than one week, but this is not the whole truth. You will still need to reinforce and deepen its benefits by applying the Five Gates Principles and Reality Rules through your daily life. The whole process of healing continues to take place for as long as you are willing to discipline yourself by living according to these self-management tools.

The immediate positive change that you will feel as you complete the Fifth Gate will give you a great degree of immediate relief because it works by helping us change our deepest beliefs about ourselves and life. These are the beliefs around which our personalities were formed as we grew up. Once we strip away many of inaccurate views and our dysfunctional adjustments to them, by seeing what really happened to us and how the world really works, the program triggers an immediate psychic realignment on both the conscious and unconscious levels. Once we experience the Five Gates Program, our surprise will not be in the dramatic changes it brings to our lives, but instead we will wonder why haven't any of the other programs we've tried worked? (If you are a psychologically buff, you will find more information about this process under the name the "Inverted Pyramid Effect.")

Why the "Peel the Onion" Method Usually Fails

Most medically based recovery approaches start by having us discuss our present situation, including the problems in our actions and beliefs. Then they work on showing us how to see the errors in our beliefs, thinking that if we can see what our therapist sees, what makes sense to our therapist will make sense to us, and we'll behave as our therapist says we should. This hope is naïve.

Eventually we start to see things in the layer that lies just below our present symptoms. We see what appears to be the immediate causes of our maladjusted thoughts, feelings and actions. This process of going deeper, one layer at a time, is called "peeling the onion." It does produce new insights, but has flaws as a method for helping us change, which we previously desired. Peeling the onion forces us to look at ourselves from the outside in, not at the deepest underlying causes that trace their origins back to our childhood.

Instead, this process brings us to layer after layer of our faulty perceptions and actions, which are more likely to depress us than produce the hope that will ignite the courage we need for change. Peeling the onion also sets up a struggle within us. Remember that denial is the logical adjustment to hopelessness. What we don't believe we can fix, we would like to deny. Peeling the onion goes against the grain of our natural defenses, and creates a numbing and discouraging experience in all but a few. Those lucky few are either not very troubled inside, or have been able to hold onto just enough self-esteem and a strong faith that the truth will set them free. People, who have suffered for a long time, have become addicted to their denial, rather than becoming empowered to face the truth.

That's why traditional therapy methods don't work well for most people, especially very troubled, intelligent people. We're far too good at inventing rationalizations to support our denial. That's why it is so hard for us to hit bottom, which is when we finally surrender our denial of the fact that we need to change. The Five Gates Program makes it unnecessary for us to wage war against our denial, but instead, provides us the solution for letting go of it after we have seen and accepted the self-assuring truths that make it unnecessary to us. The Five Gates Program successfully declares victory by going to the root of the problem, thus causing us to make the perspective changes that dissolves our denial.

The Five Gates Training Program takes much better advantage of the insights left to us by Sigmund Freud and Carl Rogers. Sigmund Freud, usually credited for the psychoanalytic method of modern psychology, provided a new perspective to the field. I like to call it the "inside-out theory." This idea says that the truths about us that someone else can see, including our therapist, have very little importance for getting us well in comparison to the truths we see about ourselves and the world.

Who Will Benefit Most?

Although the Five Gates Training Program was originally developed to help substance abusers and other addicts recover from their "using" and other addictive consequences, experience has shown that everyone who takes the Five Gates Training receives benefits that last a lifetime.

Family members of impaired individuals will find help here. Professional educators, parole officers, administrators, health care providers and counselors, as well as donors to charities supporting mental health programs and facilities, spiritual seekers and fellowship organizations will all benefit from this program's ideas and methods.

The Five Gates Training Program will help you create and maintain a higher level of spirituality by restoring your faith in your adequacy to face and manage your life. It is very effective for helping those who suffer not only from obsessive thoughts and compulsive behaviors such as those of addictions, but it has also proven effective for overcoming anxieties, depression, disorientation, attention-deficit disorder (ADD) and attention-deficit hyperactivity disorder (ADHD). Five Gates training graduates have also consistently reported substantial improvement in bipolar disorder and coping with schizophrenia. It also helps clients escape the problems of criminal recidivism, rages, resentments, self-disfigurement, eating disorders and mental blocks.

Although many of these conditions have been believed to be organic and possibly hereditary in nature, I have increasingly come to believe that the organic aspects of them are for the most part responses to dysfunctional psychological early life experiences and ideas. Several clients who have suffered from schizophrenia continue to have symptoms, but their episodes have reduced in both intensity and frequency and, equally important is the fact that they have learned to accept their condition without self-judgment and are thus able to have much better lives. The improvement in those who suffer from bipolar disorder has been even more dramatic in that the manic cycle seems to be driven by our "psychic immune system's" efforts to overcome impending severe depression. Although we have been unable to follow the lives of all our graduates with sufficient clinical thoroughness, I have not observed any reoccurrence of bipolar disorder in any of the Five Gates Graduates.

Although organically-based emotional and psychological problems are usually improved through taking the Five Gates

Training Program, in my practice it is often combined with mood-stabilizing medications from a qualified physician to temporarily or permanently restore chemical balance. This may be an important factor to help place you in a better frame of mind to work this program. But medications are not enough because some of the disabling effects of possible imbalance in one's neurological chemistry will have always brought with it an even greater need to psychologically repair one's ability to process reality in a positive way.

The more you are able to work the program honestly and devotedly, the greater and long-lasting are the benefits you'll receive. It's not necessary to be a scholar or even highly intelligent to do an excellent job of working the Five Gates Training Program. Some of those who have had excellent results were severely mentally and emotionally impaired. The more severe your disability or the greater your hope for change, the more benefit you can receive by taking the Program. Those who are able to dismiss their skepticism and be open-minded to the possibility of change have had the greatest transformational success.

How We Become Who We Are

We usually don't think about how much we are the result of where, when and by whom we were raised. If we could change that, we would be very different people. Instead, we intuitively see ourselves as a constant, familiar, self-determining person we've known for a long time. Actually, we've had much less power to choose who we would grow up to be than we may believe. Most of the deepest, long-lasting aspects of our personalities were determined during our early childhood. Back then, we were not consciously aware of how easily our environments influenced us in the beliefs that made us who we are.

When we were infants we had no wisdom, which is the knowledge of causes and effects. We only knew how we felt. We didn't even know how we were supposed to feel, only whether we liked it or not. In simple terms, babies try to avoid discomfort and experience pleasure. They can bear physical pain more than emotional pain because they usually know its source, which gives them hope it will pass eventually. But emotional pain seems to be everywhere inside all at once, as though it is completely part of us. It is. Emotional pleasure is also more intense than physical pleasure, and always brings with it a sense of security and happiness.

Our feeling of being in control of our internal world, is our greatest source of emotional pleasure. This, and the assurances we received from those who raised us, are what we used to dispel our childhood fears. Our all important self-confidence, the basis of our faith in life, is directly connected to our sense of control over ourselves, and eventually the world around us. Sometimes, our problems are caused by our unrealistic expectations concerning how much control we can really have. It is in this situation that our self-esteem can only be rescued by our new-found humility. These unrealistic expectations are taught to us and later deny us of our feelings of personal satisfaction that simply come from our managing ourselves to our best ability. When later in life other people try to tell us that we have lost control over our actions we naturally try to deny this disturbing news which is why it often takes us so long to get on a corrective path.

As we strive for more control, we constantly reach out for more understanding of our world and ourselves. In our earliest years, powerful adults gave us their beliefs and we accepted them, both because of their assurances and that most of them seemed to work. Many of their beliefs became ours, even the ones that would later prove to be wrong. When our world, based on the beliefs we were taught, seemed out of our control, our fears mounted and eventually caused our mental and emotional problems.

From the time we are infants, almost everyone tried to judge and control us. They rarely meant us any harm. They need a sense of their own empowerment and too often believe we were the source of their troubled feelings. This reassured their egos that their disappointments didn't stem from anything within themselves.

Parents taught us to see what they were taught to see, believing it was their duty to prepare us for "their world," as they understand it, which they believed would soon be ours. In our early childhoods we learn fastest. This is the period in which we can form healthy, pleasure-giving ideas, or become imprisoned with dysfunctional thinking and behavior habits. Everyone received a mixture of both. The ideas we believe from earliest childhoods are the ones that are most deeply a part of us. When these ideas don't work well, we don't either.

Sometimes, we suspect that some of our important beliefs are wrong but don't know how to correct them. We don't even know if they might be right. But we crave stability and security, which makes us protective of even wrong ideas. We become anxiety-ridden and despondent, often destructively combative and competitive when cooperation and kindness are the real answers. At these times of internal conflict, we become most vulnerable to drugs and other lies. Drugs help us believe the lies that we couldn't believe sober. Lies are our earliest and most difficult drug to kick. In desperation, we try to manage our feelings as we see we're unable to effectively manage our lives. Everyone suffers to some degree from this.

When people try to control us, they often convince themselves that they are just trying to get more pleasure and security for their own lives. But unfortunately, too often they are just trying to convince themselves that we, not they, are the source of their problems. You will rarely make a friend by pointing out this aspect of themselves, but we must avoid the trap of submitting to their judgments and accepting responsibility for their discontent. Instead, without allowing ourselves to become judgmental of them, we must devote ourselves to seeing through these dangerous traps of misdirection and false ideas.

Initially, new Five Gates graduates are taught to be less open to the ideas of others in their environment. This helps them steel themselves against the confusions and misdirection of a manipulative and often misguided world surrounding them. As they gain confidence from our practice of the Five Gates Principles and Reality Rules, they become more open to the observation and useful ideas of others. Invariably, they become beckons of light to others who are suffering from these same problems.

Our Beliefs Define Us

People come in a variety of sizes, shapes, shades, natural abilities and worldly circumstances and many from each group have happy, satisfying lives. Many do not. The most vital part of our effectiveness as people is based in our beliefs. Both our power to manage ourselves effectively and our psychologically based weaknesses stem from our beliefs, especially our beliefs about ourselves. Accurate, positive beliefs give us a positive, productive life. But, when our beliefs are wrong in important ways, this adversely affects our thoughts, feelings and our decisions. Eventually, we may suffer because we became the prisoners of our wrong beliefs Unless we make a concerted effort we don't know which of our beliefs are wrong or because they have become so deeply ingrained in our perspectives that the disorientation of abandoning them frightens us. Usually, we don't even know what they are. For this reason, we also don't know why we have the problems they created in us. In the Five Gates Program, our ability to see and evaluate our beliefs is one of the principle leverages to help us change them. We will examine the importance of our beliefs repeatedly as we train ourselves to see them so that we can become empowered to change them when we need to.

Seeing Ourselves as Knowing and Powerful Interferes With Our Growth

When we have serious character or judgment faults, we desperately do not want to see them. Anything that threatens our sense of personal effectiveness scares us, and this anxiety generates intense emotional pain. Even though we hang on to the correctness of our beliefs, if we are to grow in our understanding, we must re-examine and even revamp our beliefs, especially our inaccurate beliefs about ourselves. The contradiction between seeing ourselves as right and needing to re-examine and change our beliefs is a conflict one never quite outgrows.

We've all heard the saying, "it takes a big person to admit his mistakes." Actually, this unusual self-honesty requires a person to feel secure that he or she will improve by challenging their established beliefs. Few of us can do this voluntarily, especially when we are under emotional stresses. When we are severely stressed, we feel under siege. When we need to see the causes of our stresses most we are usually blinded by our fearful emotions. In the Five Gates Training Program we overcome this block by recording our version of the events and feelings of our history as objectively as possible, one specific question at a time. The reconciliation between our subjective interpretations of these "events" coupled with our recollection of the feelings we had at the time forces us to see the inconsistencies between the erroneous beliefs we've had as we viewed life through our child's eyes as compared to what our adult logic can show us is true. The freedom we achieve by finally getting our story "right" triggers the spiritual awakening in us that we always wanted and needed. Armed with our newly found greater understanding of ourselves and life, we finally become ready to live in harmony with the Reality Rules and Positive Principles of our program.

Our World Tries To Control Us and We It

Sometimes, our world tries to controls us in honest, straightforward ways. Society punishes those who commit violent acts or steal others' property. The world teaches us that if we want certain privileges, we must respect the rights of others and work to give something back to society to receive them. Ideally, the world is constructed for the most part, in this way. These are not the kinds of control over us that are the keys to understanding the problems addressed by this training program, even though Five Gates Training graduates live lawful, more effective and productive lives especially compared to the lives they lived before taking this program.

Sometimes, our world tries to control us in less constructive ways by trying to take advantage of our need for approval and our childhood-based inabilities to see ourselves as worthy. Our need for others' approval often results in our inability to confidently see ourselves and rely on our *own* approval (co-dependency). We all start life with a need for the approval of adults who raise us, but to the extent that this trait lives on with us in our adulthood. It makes us vulnerable to manipulation. In our early co-dependent years as infants and small children, we tend to believe what our parents and other authority figures tell us when we are good and when we are bad and expect their point of view about us to be ours as well. We craved their praise and dreaded their rebuke because we believed they knew more about us than we did. We also wanted the rewards that came with their approval. Although the material rewards may be important to us, their granting or refusal to grant their validation of us is critical to the well being of any child. Many parents have used this weapon of rejection as a weapon to control us and thus may have brought great harm. The more they disciplined us or withheld their approval from us for not being as they wished we were, the more we became emotionally affected by their views, and less confident in our views of ourselves. Co-dependence is being influenced emotionally by those who approve or disapprove of us. To some degree it remains with us throughout life, and sometimes will have the positive effect of causing us to see things we would otherwise miss. Our emotional health will depend on our achieving a balance between how we see ourselves and how others see us.

We sense when others are overly co-dependent, but usually miss this trait in ourselves. What makes co-dependence so dangerous to us is our vulnerability can become the basis of the most destructive form of interpersonal manipulations. Too often, our world tries to judge and shame us into doing what it wants by focusing on our errors and ego needs as though they were an unchangeable part of who we are. The result is that we become confused, weakened and easier to manipulate. In a wiser more loving world we reassure each other as being worthy people and simply try to share what we believe are helpful ideas. In the Five Gates Training Program, we minimize our co-dependence and refrain from taking exploitative advantage of the co-dependent tendencies of others.

Each of us grew up in a world that tries to teach us its view of what is good and bad about our behavior. In our troubled world, we have yet to discover how every person's happiness and well-being are necessary to our own.

Healthy vs. Obsessive Thoughts and Compulsive Behavior

Usually we simply try our best to do whatever we intuitively believe will feel good, right now! If we are mature and emotionally healthy we try to balance our compulsive tendency to seek immediate pleasure by also using our logic to predict the outcomes of our actions and listen to the ideas of those we trust. We all have a mental directory of the relative importance of each of these inputs to our decision making process.

The extent to which our personalities lean heavily towards giving control to our desire for short-term pleasure or avoiding pain with little concern for the long-term effects of our actions, we are compulsive. This is the natural result of our having little faith that we can help ourselves by investing in the benefits of self-discipline or restraint.

We actually have two minds; our logical mind which weighs our thoughts and actions in the way described above, and our emotional mind which is the source of our cravings and reflexes. Our emotional mind is greatly biased by our neurological chemistry and deeply ingrained beliefs, some of which may seem illogical to us now but to our frustration often have a power over us causing us to feel and do things our rational mind does not approve of. This explains why some alcoholics with end-stage liver disease keep drinking and why some can't get into an elevator without feeling a degree of panic. When we deny our emotional mind its wishes we experience cravings and may experience a struggle between what our rational and emotional minds dictate. The good news is that our emotional minds can be gradually reprogrammed by giving more weight to the dictates of our rational mind and the trust-building effects of successful experience. We can gradually learn to trust new behavior and values in this way. In the core training (first week) of the Five Gates Program, we thoroughly expose and to a significant degree we can reprogram the errors which have governed our emotional mind. In the Five Gates Life Practice we continuously try to govern our lives by positive principles and rational reality rules in order to continue to complete this process. Eventually, our core beliefs and the chemistry they generate within us will become increasingly in harmony with what our rational mind has learned to trust. Our goal is to achieve faith in positive principles, rational reality rules, and our own ability to be or do what we need to be or do to have a happy and secure life.

How Our Compulsive Natures Takes Over Our Lives

Our having prolonged unresolved suffering despite our best efforts causes us to lose faith in our ability to have a suffering-free future. We interpreted this prolonged suffering experience through the "eyes" of our earliest logical tool, our belief that our future will resemble our past. We concluded that through our present actions, we could do little to secure a much-improved future. This is the dilemma that every addict faces in his or her psychologically based cravings.When we are depressed and compulsive, we become fatalistic and conclude that because we feel miserable today, have been miserable so far, despite our efforts at times to improve our situations, we will feel miserable tomorrow and indefinitely. This makes us believe that the best chance we have for any happiness at all is to give in to our emotional mind which craves immediate relief instead of believing in the promises that self-restraint will give us what we want and need.

Once defeated, we stop improving our situation because we believe it will hurt us less. To lose our struggle uncontested appears a better outcome than if we had tried our best and lost anyway. If we try hard and lose, we feel like failures. This usually happens because we were never taught that trying our best is success in itself. To feel better about not trying to solve our problem, we may try to fool ourselves by saying, "If I wanted to, I could win." But, this doesn't work either. When we stop trying, we know we will continue to suffer, usually worse than before, and begin to dread the future altogether. Depression like this is the root cause of our inability to try to improve.

In the Five Gates Philosophy we say that anxiety (fear) - hope = depression. In our weakened state of depression, we desperately reach out for quick fixes to soothe the pain of our anxiety. Compulsive behavior is the result. Some of us were taught in early childhood that worry (an expression of fear) and not just caution, is necessary to keep us safe. If we were raised this way we became addicted to negative thoughts that further drove our anxieties to constantly force us to look at life as dangerous or negative to us. As this habitual way of thinking deepened within us, we eventually found that our inability to help ourselves from becoming anxiety-ridden made us depressed.

In my practice, I have discovered that most people who were believed to have a hereditary predisposition to anxiety and depression could usually overcome these problems by simply changing their beliefs about themselves and life. When they went to their physician they were asked if either of their parents also suffered from this problem, and if so their problem was written off as "running in the family," and could probably be fixed with the proper medications. The real problem is that in their early childhood they were taught to see themselves and life in ways that were anxiety-producing resulting in depression. The causes of depression and not only the symptoms can almost always be resolved through this program.

I have often been asked why I don't believe in the hereditary nature of addictions, anxiety disorder or depression. The truth is I don't really know, but I have never had a client who seeming predisposition toward these problems could not be explained by our discovery of how he or she grew up to be who they are as it was revealed in their Fifth Gate journey. In other words I have yet to find the well-adjusted child of well-adjusted parents who upon exposure to alcohol and no other negative emotional problems suddenly found him or herself addicted to alcohol, unexplainably anxiety ridden or severely depressed. If these afflictions were hereditary I should have found many. On the other hand some people may experience greater pleasure or euphoria when exposed to the same amount of certain stimulations and may therefore find it harder to keep their rational mind in control of their emotional mind particularly in times of stress.

More on Our Co-Dependent Natures

To the extent that we make decisions based on our own logic, we are mature. To the degree we are motivated to seek the approval of others to substitute for our ability to reassure ourselves, we are deficit co-dependent. A high degree of co-dependence is natural, logical, and useful to small children, since their experiences and abilities to make good choices are not yet well developed. Adolescence is a time for gaining our self-esteem through greater self-reliance. Adolescents may even reject or claim to reject the praise or criticisms from authority figures to reassure themselves of their independence. Mature adults approach this need in a more objective and balanced way. As our Fifth Gate journey teaches us to see life and ourselves more clearly, we shed our deficit co-dependency. This factor alone can provide us the positive energy to break the hold of our compulsively driven anxiety and depression.

Overcoming Low Self-Esteem

From infancy our world has used our need to feel secure as a tool to control us by manipulating our *perceptions of our abilities to do what we need to have a happy and secure life (self-esteem)*. At the beginning of our lives, we know little and have little power to meet the simplest of our needs. At this time, our minds are sharp, receptive and not as cluttered with irrelevancies as they later become. As we venture forth into a more complex life cluttered by symbols for success and danger, these abilities might serve some use. But at our earliest ages, we rationally conclude we must take advice from authority figures. We correctly assume they know more about life than we do. When we accept their wisdom and seek their approval without challenge, this orientation is called co-dependence. We believe they know who we are and how we should be, as well as what we should or should not do.

As we mature in healthy ways, we begin to trust our own opinions on things, especially about ourselves. In adolescence, we challenge authority figures, often for the sake of asserting our independence, even though we are not nearly as self-sufficient as we believe. Later, we simply accept responsibility for being adults and make our opinions with a more balanced view, comfortable using the wisdom of others as well.

If we grew up emotionally troubled and confused, we tend to be unable to grow out of our childhood co-dependencies or our adolescent need to reject even wise authorities. Then the co-dependencies we take into our adult years set us up for manipulation and painful self-doubts. Those who have taken the Five Gates Training Program achieve greater self-empowerment by knowing how to balance their relationships with themselves and their worlds. As their anxieties rapidly fade, they take away with them the cravings for drugs and self-deception. This kind of fundamental approach towards healing the whole person is the only kind of treatment program that can work.

Feelings

We program computers to carry out our instructions in a very narrow set of situations. We call this a program. Human beings operate by programs too, but ours are far more complex, and so far no computer experiences feelings which are an exclusive experience of living things. We notice that at times there is a conflict between our rational mind and our emotional mind. This means that they are running different programs even though they are interconnected. The connections are in our core beliefs and our brain chemistry. Our core beliefs not only provides a platform from which our logic can operate, but also helps us interpret what's going on which touches us emotionally. Our neurological chemistry not only provides the energy on which our logic can operate, but gives us an emotional response which is a logic unto itself. Eventually, our scientists will probably even make this distinction much less separate and mysterious as they continue to better simulate the operations of living things inside computers.

Our feelings are a response to two kinds of stimulation. The first is our beliefs about what is going on with something we care about, and the second is our neurological chemistry or physical processes that may bring with them sensations, and even the stimulation of nerves that can make us euphoric, anxiety-ridden, manic, or depressed. Here, we want to talk about the feelings we get from our beliefs, and further separate those into two kinds:

our long-term beliefs, and our beliefs about a particular situation in the moment.

Love and Fear— Opposing Forces

Fear shrinks our world and locks us isolated inside of ourselves. Love expands our world and releases us to feel the joy of our connections with "The All" which some define as God. The Five Gates Training reduces our fears and opens us up to our natural ability to feel connected and happy. The defeat of fears is faith which is the mother of love and our emotional health.

In Alcoholics Anonymous (AA) and other fellowship groups, people will say that if you are angry you need to look at what you fear. You have taken your fear and by pointing to a cause outside yourself, you have converted your fear into the feeling we call anger. If we find we can tempt someone intensely, our advisors will tell us that we should be on the lookout for ways in which that person resembles a part of ourselves we don't like. But, what about love?

Everyone wants to be loved. When we are honest with ourselves, being loved means that somehow we will be more secure, because whoever loves us will be helpful to us more than those who do not. But this isn't the most important thing about love.

When we love, it's a thrilling and uplifting experience. Some people will argue with this, saying they have suffered in misery by loving others to their detriment. But what they probably mean is they have been addicted to a kind of dysfunctional relationship that they have mistakenly called love. People also talk about conditional and unconditional love. Love is generally a topic of conversation about which people seem to have the greatest misunderstanding.

First, we need to take a look at what we mean when we say love. Love is a feeling, not a decision. Love is a positive feeling, never a negative feeling. When we stop to take a look at what we really mean by the feeling of love, we may notice that love inspires us to be helpful or protective to that which we love. What does that mean? It means that when we think deeply about what we love and about what is important to us, what we love we have made part of ourselves. Love doesn't require the permission of that which we love. Our love is about no one's feelings but our own. That's why love is always unconditional. By conditional love, people are referring to a deal, not love.

Much has been written on this key aspect of what we must do in order to guide ourselves to higher and more joyful functioning. We must know when and why we are troubled. But, most sources don't address how important it is to know when and why we are joyful, what turns us on.

A profound philosopher once said that one match lit in a dark room will chase away a lot of darkness. So also will we heal amazingly fast if we can not only eliminate what troubles us, but also embrace what gives us joy. Expressing our love for all things by being of service to this world will give us great pleasure. The reason we have a distinct section to learn how to give ourselves pleasure from life at the conclusion of our Fifth Gate is because those of us who have experienced suffering and broken lives either lost or never really knew how to do this for ourselves. When you don't have a method of taking yourself into a happier space, when the shoes of life get tight, you have no defense against your pain becoming suffering, and your suffering becoming insanity.

As we consider the causes of our feelings and the importance of managing our feelings, it becomes obvious that the seemingly simple act of knowing how we feel at any given moment can be very important. This job only seems simple, because when we are not happy with life and ourselves, we often lie to ourselves about the way we feel. We mistake fear for anger and outrage. We mistake lust for love. We mistake our attempt at righting injustice for our rationalizations for what we want to do that has nothing to do with justice at all. We use these self-deceptions as a mistaken way to make us feel better about our unhappiness, which is usually caused by our fears. Since this process is natural to our ego's self-defense system, we need a reliable method for seeing through our smoke and mirrors, straight to the facts of what's really going on deeper inside us.

We can do this by first accepting that all our negative feelings are destructive to us and seduce us into lying to ourselves. When we are afraid, we invent all kinds of reactions to deal with the inevitable low self-esteem (dreading our lives), and the pain, anxiety and sometimes-even depression that follow. Anytime we are scared, angry, accusatory, hating, judging or anything else that is negative, we need to be certain that somewhere underneath is our fear that we are inadequate, and we are going to suffer a tragic loss. The exception to this rule is worth knowing, but we should not give it too much importance. Sometimes, we pick up bad habits of being judgmental or pretending to be more outraged and angry than we are because we were told that we are supposed to feel that way in certain situations. The truth is that little bothers the happy person because little worries the happy person. We all know there are plenty of disturbed people in this world who do all kinds of destructive things. Those of us who have finally achieved enough balance in our perspective say to ourselves "why me?" "Why not me!?" or "what goes around comes around!"

In the Five Gates Training Program, we learn that we must round up "the usual psychic suspects" in connection with any of our negative feelings. But we must learn to do this for ourselves because when other people try to do this for us, our ego defense system will either make us argumentative or needlessly depressed, because we are co-dependent. We learn to live now by reassuring ourselves that our only real job is to decide on what to do and then do it. Everything else knocking at our psychic door is a dangerous and misleading self-deception.

All of our thoughts of and feelings of revenge or wishing bad will on anyone are always misguided. Are we really better off when our "enemies" suffer? Are we really better people when others believe what isn't true of us in order that we can have their praise? Does our acquiring money or status really make us better people? Who among us can really say that we have rejected the seductive idea that the world's rewards given to us may be unjust? Don't we always congratulate ourselves anytime things turn out well for us, whether our good fortune was really caused by us or not? When we learn to manage ourselves in the present to our best ability, none of this matters to us. We must remind ourselves that their praise, admiration, and love belong to them and our self-respect (self-esteem) belongs to us! When we learn to think this way, it also shields us from the psychologically harmful effects of our "bad breaks." Our life effectiveness zooms!

Self-Knowing Begins Our Journey

Remember the image of ourselves as infants? Back then we didn't know anything about causes and effects? Didn't we blame ourselves for all our pain and discomfort and congratulate ourselves for all our pleasure? We had no way of knowing what brought these feelings upon us, but we had little to do with what was causing our pain or pleasure. Despite this, those early experiences told us how much we loved our lives and ourselves (same thing), and looked forward to what we could predictably see ahead of us, or how much we would grow up dreading the roads that lie ahead. Now that we know and can learn much more about how the world and we work, it's time for us to outgrow our childish ways of thinking. Now we need more wisdom which is the knowledge of causes and effects.

The answer to the challenge of reading our feelings is to change the question instead of investing ourselves and becoming masters of the answers we want to believe. We need to learn to ground our feelings in truths. We must believe the philosopher's who have told us, "The Truth Shall Set Us Free." When we are suffering and clinging to our addictions, we lack faith that we will find solutions in truth. This is our dilemma; what we need most we find ourselves unable to trust.

Simple logic reinforces one of the key teachings of the Five Gates Training Program, that we have only one job in life: to manage ourselves the best we can in the present! Everything else we can or should do for ourselves is a lie. Once we come to believe this, it all gets a lot easier. All negative thoughts we have are based on lies. Suppose we have cancer. Will fear of death make us enjoy what remains of our lives, or heal us from the cancer any sooner or better? No. Therefore, this fear is destructive, and even though it may be incredibly hard to rise above it, especially in this example, doing so will give us the best possible result.

Anytime we feel a negative feeling, we have only to do two things. First, we should try to see if there is an obvious cause, based on one's lack of ability to face the future. Our only job in life is to manage ourselves the best we can in the only thing we have, the present. If we know in our hearts that this is the best we can do for ourselves, what we thought was a deceptively simple task, reading our feelings, can now become a genuinely simple task by following the Five Gates Training Program for managing our lives. Once we get into the habit of living in the Five Gates, the challenge of managing our feelings can be overcome easily. We can even, at times, accept that we have been unable to read our inner feelings well enough to be sure exactly what is going on inside ourselves. We can rescue ourselves anyway, by simply taking an "action intervention" on ourselves by managing our thoughts in the present. Invariably, I have found that once I do this, the solution to the mystery of what is going on inside me rises to the surface almost at once.

The physical world seems very tangible and immediate, so we tend to trust it more than other stimuli. Most often, we overestimate the effects of the physical and don't clearly see the causes and effects of our beliefs. From the beginning of our first awareness, we construct a version of reality that tells us who we are, who we need to be, what we need to do, and what we need to fear. Even though we learned these most basic ideas in childhood, when we co-dependently "swallowed whole" the ideas of the world in which were raised, we still think of these ideas as being our own. These "core beliefs" shape our perceptions now.

Our version of history is the place we keep our self-image, including our abilities, limitations and opportunities. We see ourselves as a composite of our history. In order for us to change and grow, we need to reinterpret our histories so that we can see that we have attainable possibilities that transcend them. This is the source of our hope and growth.

Usually, we're not consciously aware of our assumptions that we see life this way, as the sum of useless fears and wrong ideas we were spoon-fed as children. These fears and ideas confuse us, and make us needlessly vulnerable to debilitating emotional pain and misdirection of our efforts.

Intuitively, we know that we need to feel safe or we will suffer the pains of anxieties, and so we do our best to build for ourselves a belief system, a view of ourselves and life that helps us believe in our safety. This fortress of belief in our adequacy is the foundation of our faith. Faith, in this sense, is what we believe without questioning. Our greatest goal in the Five Gate Training Program is achieved through our re-examining our lives and our worlds and learning new ideas that will allow us to achieve a faith which sustains our belief in our ability to be adequate to life's challenges. This will always require that we see our purpose and opportunities in new ways.

When new experiences or information challenges our self-beliefs, we use or rework our beliefs to restore faith in our ability to have a safe, pleasurable life. All of us, at times, use comfortable lies in order to cope with life. For most of us, much of the time, this works to a sufficient degree, and our fears do not take over our lives. Though we may not be joyful, we manage to balance our beliefs about reality so that we function adequately.

In addition, when we find ourselves unable to reconcile our need to feel safe with what we believe are facts that contradict our faith, and threaten our safety, we feel pain and anxiety. When the pain goes on without relief long enough, we lose our faith that it will ever leave us, and we become depressed Long-term pain becomes suffering and eventually depression, if not relieved by our ability to reconcile it with a life-view that helps us see our safety. Our ideas of our worthiness are just ideas we use to convince ourselves we're safe. We want to believe we can keep ourselves from external causes of danger by being worthy of a "good" life.

Balancing Our Disappointments

As we mature we also learn that "bad things happen to good people," and some who seem unworthy are rewarded with many pleasures we want for ourselves, and may have found unattainable. In order to give ourselves the best fortress of faith and functionality, we need a belief system that helps us see that we hold power and have a reliable method for giving ourselves the pleasures of a good life. Most of all we need a new definition of self-adequacy which is tied to us and not the world.

The Five Gates Training Program is a path to delivering that essential power to ourselves. We accomplish this by doing four things:

1. We see and accept that we are suffering because of our mistaken beliefs, especially our unrealistic expectations. These are the causes of our needless fears and the resulting suffering.

2. We commit ourselves to learn to trust in a new, more effective way of seeing ourselves and our world.

3. We see and accept that our limitations are not our shortcomings. This places our emphasis on managing ourselves instead of judging ourselves.

4. We practice the Five Gates as our lifestyle (Life Practice). This helps us recondition ourselves not to trust in our failed beliefs and learn to trust in the positive principles and reality rules of The Five Gates Program.

If we stay determined to bring about these changes in ourselves through study, meditation, analytical thought and practice, we will build a new and much more pleasurable, productive life.

Free Will and Foolish Behavior

We all tend to fall into the trap of believing that what we understand immediately becomes a part of us. Sometimes, we extend this assumption to others. We ask them, "Don't you know that drugs are bad for you?" or "Don't you know smoking cigarettes will give you cancer?" It's as if we believe that everyone has completely free will, meaning that once they see it in their logical minds, they can do whatever it takes to have the best outcome. We can do all our homework, stop smoking cigarettes, stop getting into problem relationships, stop everything that is not good for us, and start everything that is the best for us. Of course, we believe that everyone else can, could or should do that, too. The problem is that this reasoning is the dictate of our rational mind, which does not take into account our emotional mind, which also needs reprogramming that will take longer than simply seeing logical truths. We begin that process in our Fourth and Fifth Gates which enables us to access our core beliefs through which we can begin the process of changing our emotional mind so that it becomes more in harmony with our rational mind.

What we think and what we know are not exactly the same things. What we think is logical; we believed that what has happened before will happen again, and what has solved our problems before will solve our problems now. This does not always make sense because circumstances may not be the same as before. Somehow we know we are not immortal. Nothing we will do will cause us to stay healthy or alive indefinitely, or even for all that long. But, what we have is real faith in the importance of what will make us feel better. We'll give almost anything to have that feeling, even give our tomorrows, our good name or our civil freedoms. The people in jail know crime doesn't pay, but for some people doing what will diminish them later feels good at the moment they do it. Examples of this are smoking, chocolate nut sundaes, sex with our neighbor's spouse, driving over 100 miles an hour and a whole lot of other things are dangerous or bad for us, even though they might seem to feel good at the time. If we want to start living wisely, we'll need to understand that what is good for us is also good *to* us. We can do this in the Five Gates Life Practice, since by living in an enlightened way we will derive pleasures and joys we never knew existed when we were driven like fools, consuming our very opportunity for life.

Our Ego Seduces Us to Believe in Our Willpower

Another misguided way we approach our problems takes place when we decide that, through our willpower, we are going to stop ourselves from doing things that have a strong emotional hold on us. The world has told us that we can "Just Say No." But we know that the present is the inescapable and perfectly logical result of the past. Therefore, we must attack our problems of the future by removing their causes in the present.

Can we "just say no" to lies, drugs, gambling, dysfunctional relationships and laziness? Can we place ourselves above all these things once they have taken hold of our willpower? Once they have taken over our willpower in a deep-seated part of ourselves, they have become a part of us, and even though we usually do not like to admit it or cannot see this truth, a deeply rooted part of us believes we need them to give us something we want or need. This is what we must change in ourselves.

If we were at peace with ourselves, we would have everything we need, but not necessarily everything we want for our future. The way to diffuse our cravings for dysfunctional and unproductive behavior is to achieve internal peace. It is only by going to those deep-seated parts of ourselves and making the changes in our belief systems that we can truly free ourselves from their hold on us. The Five Gates Training Program has stood alone in its ability to rapidly take us to those deeply buried centers of wrong beliefs and change them to positive beliefs.

Anger is a Strong Motivator, But Love Is Stronger

Can we say that we are truly happy if we are angry? We must examine the sources and nature of our anger. At our deepest levels we know that anger is not really about anyone but us. What has happened is that we believe things should be different than they are. We believe that we, or others, must be different, and naturally give in to our temptation to focus our problem on someone else's actions. But we never had any power over who they are, or even over the world that shaped us into who we are. Most people who do negative things do so because they are misguided, not because they have evil intentions. Even those whom we think of the worst criminals of the 20th century, such as Stalin and Hitler had idealistic beliefs that underlie their brutal decisions and actions. The parents of many disabled people who trace their problems to their childhood probably thought that their form of discipline and guidance would be good for their child and not disabling. Often, people act out under the control of their frustrations even when they know under ordinary circumstances that those actions are destructive. They simply can't find the wisdom or inner strength to get outside of themselves sufficiently to take responsibility with the effects of what they are doing under severe stress. It is not our job to judge them or ourselves, or believe we should be someone different than who we are. Our job is to help us become more positively empowered and possibly help them, which is another way of helping ourselves.

But, how many of us really think that way, or think that way when someone does something that hurts us? If we get angry, we have taken the bait and allowed their misguided actions to steal our happiness. For the sake of our happiness, we need more wisdom. We need to accept that everything has a cause and the present is the inevitable result of the past, therefore it is perfect for now. This wisdom is usually reserved as a graduate exercise in the Five Gates Training Program. With it, we can focus ourselves sharply in the present and dedicate ourselves to ideas and actions that are positive.

Getting Smarter is Not Enough — We Must Vicariously Relive Our Life's "Movie Script"

Although getting smarter about the implications of our thoughts, feelings and actions may help us correct those that are less deep-seated, the real teacher for us is what we can learn from life itself, especially our own lives. Every problem we have today is caused by the false beliefs we have today. The problem, if we suffer from anxiety, depression, or low self-esteem and a lack of positive motivation, is that we were present for the highly realistic movie called "Our Life." While we lived it, we learned too many wrong negative and too few right positive things. But no classroom logic or repetition of contradictions can ever change them. We need to experience a more positive "movie script" of our lives.

In the Fourth and Fifth Gates, we successfully change our wrong dysfunctional beliefs by vicariously reliving and re-examining those parts of our "movie script" from which we drew the wrong conclusions. Each important dysfunctional belief we change triggers a chain reaction of deep healing with us (spiritual awakening). In psychology, this is called the inverted pyramid effect. Once we change any deep-seated belief, almost instantly a whole stacked array of wrong conclusions and resulting dysfunctional personality problems that depended upon that wrong belief are reversed. This is so powerful that at the conclusion of the Fifth Gate, more than 95 percent of Five Gates graduates noticeably glow with the powerful effect of their healing. More than 80 percent of Five Gates graduates achieve a lasting, positive change in every aspect of their lives and a greatly improved spiritual condition.

Parents and Loved Ones Are a Special Challenge for Us

For those who are least personally connected to us, their judgments and manipulations are easier to avoid. In the cases of our parents and those closest to us, it's harder for them to avoid being judgmental, especially when they believe we are making serious or frequent errors of judgment. If those who raised us or have been closest to us were to accept responsibility for their part in creating who we are, or even for having unwittingly overlooked our more serious faults, they would also, at times, have to painfully judge themselves as inadequate. We all try to avoid doing that.

For this reason, they need to believe, and want us to believe, that we've always had more control over what we feel, believe and do than what we really did have. At the same time, our special codependent and other emotional connections with them have made us more vulnerable to blindly accepting their point of view about us. Many times people, even Five Gates graduates, face a special challenge in dealing with parents and other loved ones than they do in effectively dealing with the rest of their environments. When this happens to Five Gates graduates we correct this problem by refocusing on our program repeatedly as we monitor ourselves in the Five Gates Life Practice.

We are not suggesting that parents and other loved ones have a special destructive agenda in trying to prevent us from achieving greater self-empowerment. As a general rule, parents really mean well even when they say or do things that will cause their child to feel inadequate. Their motive is to inspire or discipline their child into taking more constructive actions on their own behalf. Even when their motives are not so pure, the real objective is to get the child better behaved so the parents are not greatly inconvenienced. Rarely is a parent's motive to hurt his or her child. Parents have to deal also with the competition inherent in earning a living and angling for worldly advantages. They are limited by how their parents raised them and how they were taught to see themselves. Through generation after generation, what they experienced and believed became the basis of what we experienced and believed, and eventually defined us. Too often, our parents didn't know or forgot to tell us that the most important purpose of their and our lives was to be happy.

Unfortunately, these natural judgmental tendencies are the major reason that so many of us grow up feeling needlessly inadequate, anxiety-ridden or depressed. At the bottom line, the roots of our anxieties and depressions stem from our having been taught to judge ourselves as inadequate to do our jobs in life. Some of us were taught to see ourselves as permanently inadequate. When we believe this, it is our most dangerous and destructive handicap in life. As long as we are focused on judging ourselves instead of assessing the wisdom of our beliefs, feelings and actions, with a view toward improving them, we are doomed to feel insecure, instead of motivated positively and hopefully. In the Five Gates Training Program, we rid ourselves of this problem. We are taught to see ourselves more accurately, by reprocessing the conclusions we drew from our earliest experiences. The Five Gates Program teaches us how to make accurate assessments, but not to judge ourselves or others.

Insanity

This can be a cruel, misleading and depersonalizing term since it directs us to no real understanding of anyone or positive action at all, but instead it labels some people as invalid by focusing on problems and not their solutions. Our experience is that all people are valid, but at times some of us have been misguided in extreme ways. Confused and misguided are positive terms when they direct us towards learning and we search out, find, and correct the causes. Labeling people is destructive of their self-esteem, but offering guidance to those whose judgments and actions have brought them suffering is constructive for them and for us.

A very accomplished psychiatrist once told me that the label "insane" is actually a political statement, since it doesn't tell you anything specific about a person's condition except that they appear to think ineffectively outside of the norms. The reason our enlightened psychiatrist said that insane is a political word, is that its use serves only to justify our condemnation, most likely for the purpose of taking away their civil rights instead of helping them. When abnormal thinking has positive results, we call it genius or when they are powerful in other ways we say they are eccentric.

In the Five Gates Program most who come to us for help are able to overcome their dysfunctional thinking to such a degree that the term insane will no longer apply to them. We find the key causes and correct them to the degree possible. Once people begin to experience progress in this positive direction it generates in them the hope and courage they have needed to heal themselves. We look at this miracle as the real goal and never to "insanity" as a useful label for anything accept extreme emotional disturbance brought on by profoundly misdirected thoughts which can be corrected once we find the keys to their causes. We were pleasantly surprised to discover that many schizophrenics, even when their schizophrenic symptoms could only be reduced in frequency and intensity became able to think outside of their hallucinations well enough to see them for what they were. We encourage them when appropriate to laugh about them saying "My life is more interesting than most." Of course there will always be those too unable to take the Five Gates Training, but we have found these to be very few.

Spiritual Programs Throughout Time

Most modern spiritual teachings tell us many of the same things: to focus in the present, unload our judgments and resentments in favor of self-management and acceptance, live on the positive side of life's options by being generous, loving and constructive. Doing these things is supposed to reflect back on you the light you bring to it. The same advice exists in some of the older spiritual regimes as well: Hindus, Jews (including the teachings of Jesus), Toltecs, Buddhists, Pagans and others are all admonished on the virtues of processing life from a perspective of being focused in the present, with a loving embrace towards all of creation. The problem is that none of these fine teachings tell us how we can quickly change from being the fear-ridden person we are, to some extent, grew up to be, to being the more open, loving person whose lack of fear has opened up one's talents and pleasures. All spiritual programs, except those that believe your virtue and salvation are delivered by an outside magical power, say that if you keep studying, praying and doing positive deeds, you will eventually be transformed by this process into the more desirable you. The methods of the Five Gates Training Program can help you do the majority of this job, virtually overnight, in less than a week.

We Are One — Not Separate

The logically obvious, but not always easy to accept truth is that we are all so interconnected that, to some degree, we are all a part of why each of us is who we are, and a part of what each of us has or has not yet done. The more wisdom we've had, the more responsible we are. The greatest and most destructive lies we are taught to believe come from our mistaken faith in our separateness. Our inability to see and accept our connections is at the root of almost all our personal and social dysfunctions. It generates our fears and most of our destructive waste.

In the long run, we will have no security or happiness as long as our neighbors harbor pain and suffering, self-doubts and confusions. Just accepting our involvement, and dedicating ourselves to the world's healing, will heal us. As the Fourth and Fifth Gates of our program free us from the destructive ideas that caused our anxieties, obsessions, depressions, and compulsions, we find it easier to continue our positive journey and feelings of empowerment by dedicating ourselves to the help of others. This is the central focus of the Five Gates Life Practice.

Faith is the Answer

"We all have some degree of faith in something or we would be driven mad by our fears. We have faith that the sun will rise in the morning and the Earth's gravity will keep us flying off into space. But do we have faith that we can be or do what we need to be or do to have a happy and secure life? This is the faith we need and once we have it the steps to wellness are easy to take." (From *Recover With Me,* © 1998, Lynn Kesselman, Recovery Press)

Why is Faith So Important to Us?

We have faith in anything we believe without questioning. Faith that things will turn out fine for us is the opposite of fear, and fear is the driving force behind our anxieties, depression, and eventually emotional disorders and, for some of us, our insanities. In the Five Gates Program we call these the "children of fear." Our addictions, including our addiction to negative thoughts and actions, are symptoms caused by our craving to escape the pains of our fears. We actually use our addictions to protect us against the even greater despondencies and insanities we intuitively believe our unresolved problems and fears would cause in us.

When we are anxiety-ridden, we reflexively put our faith in the belief that worry, and, not just caution, will keep us safe from our problems. This is a prime example of the how faith can have a dark side. A person who does irrationally repetitive things like washing their hands or cleaning their homes when they are not dirty, may have obsessive-compulsive disorder. When we do things like this, we are obsessed with the irrational thought that instead of facing our problems, we need to escape them artificially by keeping our minds preoccupied with substitutes for our worry. Our addictions are the compulsive things we use to run away from life, instead of dealing with it head-on. We then lie to ourselves as we make the leap of faith that our compulsive actions will actually keep us safe from our troubles. This is how our faith in our inability to solve our real problems brings us suffering, emotional and mental disorders, and prevents us from finding real solutions to life's challenges.

We will be sane, at peace, and happy if we can find faith in the positive side of our lives; faith that by being and doing what we need to be or do, the world will be most likely to reward us for our good intentions and decisions. Remember, that "bad" things still happen to "good" people, but just not as often. Our need for all of our maladjustments would be lifted, even though it may take some time and effort for us to clear up our old habits. This is done by seeing them for what they are and rejecting them as they present themselves as false solutions to our real problems. As we heal, they lose their hold on us.

Do We Need More than Faith?

Although our faith that life will turn out fine for us will take away our anxieties for the moment in which we experience it, our faith can be shaken when we have placed our faith in beliefs and actions that do not work in the real world. This is why we need wisdom, and a commitment to keep trying to learn more from our experience and the experience of others. We need faith that we can learn the important things we do not know about how to live life well. But we need even more than this. We need to accept that our earlier lives taught us to have faith in beliefs that didn't work. Our old beliefs will not simply surrender when we see them as wrong. To break their hold on us, we must learn new ones for which we have just enough confidence. As we see our new more positive principles more successfully, we gain faith in them to try living by them. The more desperate we were, the easier it will be to abandon our old dysfunctional beliefs once we begin to gain confidence in new ones. This is a major part of our job in retraining ourselves to live more empowered and happier lives based on more positive perspectives and actions.

As we journey through the Five Gates, we will loosen the grip that our old dysfunctional ideas had on us. At the same time, it will give us positive principles which are easily understood for us to try out so that we can experience a deepening faith in them as our life experiences show us that they are working. This may sound like a long and difficult process. The practicality of the Five Gates Training Program is that you can actually launch yourself on this positive and rewarding path quickly. You will know that the positive principles of the Five Gates are right for you because you will see encouraging results immediately upon your completion of the Fifth Gate.

Religions, Faith and God

For some, religions provide many of the same spiritual benefits of the Five Gates Training Program. In a sense, each religion is a program of recovery. The Program does not conflict with any constructive and positive views of any major religion of which I am aware. There are, however, important differences.

All religions tell us that we need faith to give us the needed strength to function well in life. When they give hope to a spiritually bankrupt person, they will take away that person's anxieties and depression. But, when a religion is based on blind faith and an assurance that this person will have a good life once they give their faith to the belief of that religion, it is necessary that the believer continue to experience a good life or that person will lose his faith and once again fall prey to the ravages of anxiety, fear, and despair. This is an impossibly difficult test for any religion that is rooted in superstition, since life itself as it reveals our successful and unsuccessful beliefs will always be the litmus test of our spiritual condition. Their positive principles and reality rules must prove worthy of a person's faith as life itself reveals their truth. If they fail, that person will be more confused and despondent than ever.

Most modern and ancient spiritual teachings tell us many of the same things: to focus in the present, reject our judgments and resentments in favor of self-management and acceptance, live on the positive side of life's choices, be generous, loving, constructive and your life will reflect back the light you bring to it. All the great spiritual teachings of this world throughout every epoch have universally informed humans on the virtues of processing life focused on the present, with a loving embrace towards all creation.

The problem is that none of these fine teachings tell us how we can quickly, without relying upon superstition, change from being the fear-ridden, judgmental person we are, to being the more open, loving person whose spiritual fullness has opened up his or her talents and pleasures beyond anything possible for most of us today. All spiritual programs, except those that believe that your virtue and salvation are delivered by an outside magical power, say that if you keep studying, praying and doing positive deeds, you will eventually be transformed by this process into a more effective, happier you.

The method of the Five Gates Training Program can help you do much of this job more quickly because it focuses us on the basic ways by which we process reality itself. The Church of Religious Science, Hindu Ashrams, Judaism (including the teachings of Jesus), Alcoholics Anonymous and many others to some extent hold similar truths to healing the spirit.

Spiritual Bankruptcy

Bill Wilson, the co-founder of AA said (paraphrased), "I am as far away from my next drink as my spiritual condition is good." He goes on to describe alcoholism as caused by "Spiritual Bankruptcy." In the Five Gates Program we agree that drinking alcoholics are suffering from spiritual bankruptcy, but we see spiritual bankruptcy as being caused by the bankruptcy or absence of faith.

The Five Gates Program is Rooted in Biblical Messages

The Jewish Bible (Torah), or Old Testament, describes the first man, Adam as living idyllically happy until he ate the forbidden (not good for us) fruit of the tree of knowing to judge good from evil. Our desire and even our belief that we can know what things should and should not be is at the base of our aspirations to improve our world. This is an idea we accept without question. On the other hand, our dissatisfaction with what exists in the present is at the root of our acquired emotional and mental problems, and many of our social injustices and atrocities. When we judge the past or the present we're judging the same reality because the present is the inescapable result of everything in the past. It is unchangeable and therefore it cannot help us in any way to judge it as bad. Our dissatisfaction with some aspects of the present gives us the motivation to work toward what we believe will be a better future. Thus, this is not an expectation but a hope and does us good, not harm. We accept that we can never know the future, and that the present, for now, has turned out perfectly, even though in some ways we may not be satisfied with it. Our dissatisfaction with the past and therefore the present is our problem since it has no use in the present since the present is only good for taking actions to improve the future. Living in our past dissatisfactions will likely distract us from living in the present solutions.

The disappointing messages from the past and present sometimes tell us that we were inadequate to meet life's challenges. It reasons that we were always the result of the forces acting upon us and within us, and, therefore, we wish to improve, but not reject ourselves or anyone else over past or present disappointments. Our judgments prevent us from living constructively in the present, and this cripples our ability to work toward a future we believe will bring us greater satisfaction. We must forgive (understand and accept) all others and ourselves so we can be free and happy in our efforts to move toward a future we like.

Five Gates Graduates Place Their Faith in Positive Intentions and Acceptance of Reality

Successful Five Gates graduates maintain their spiritual condition through beliefs that are anchored in reality and the nature of creation (reality) itself. We accept that we can never know the future and therefore must have no expectations of it. Our faith is rooted in our belief that we will always enjoy life more by living it in accordance with positive principles, accepting without judgment that reality is God's will or the ultimate order of the universe. We expect the world outside us to give us disappointments, but we see our disappointments stemming from our unrealistic expectations and not with any imperfections in reality. This does not mean we are fatalistic since we strive in the present to help shape a future we believe will be to our liking. We simply accept that the past is unchangeable, and therefore the present must be accepted without complaint. Of course, this is perfection which none of us truly achieves.

For us, God is a way of describing all that has brought this world into being in such a way that if we've got our reality rules perfectly aligned with the truth of how the world really is, we are in touch with God's will. We also believe in a positive world, because we see that positive principles work better than negative ones to keep us happy and empowered. This tells us we have a loving God. But we do not ask any Five Gates Trainer or graduate to believe in a God of any kind, but only a reality that responds best to positive thoughts and actions.

PART TWO

PREPARING FOR THE JOURNEY
OF THE FIVE GATES

How Do We Know if We Need This Journey?

The insight we can gain here is very critical to our whole process of self-redevelopment. How much dedication and focus can we give to a program that requires us to re-examine our deepest beliefs, the ones that hold our entire view of reality together? If we don't know how much we need to do for our own sakes, it's hard to be objective about seeing the flaws in our views, since they required that we believe them more than by their objective truth. In order to make this process more objective, it's best for us to examine a checklist to see how well our views, and the behavior that flows from them, are giving us a good life.

Evaluate your present condition as honestly as you can by answering the following questions and giving each one a numerical assessment which you will find in the directions. This is not a medically or scientifically proven test, but simply an overall way of looking at your self as you are before taking the journey of the Five Gates Training. You may want to return to this section periodically after you've completed your Fifth Gate. Keep a running score of each of the four sets of questions. At the end we will share with you what experience has taught us about the meaning of your score.

These tests are not medical. YOU SHOULD CONSULT WITH YOUR PHYSICIAN IN ORDER TO DETERMINE IF THESE RESULTS ARE ACCURATE TO YOUR CONDITION.

1. Do I have anxieties? *Anxieties result from unproductive fears.*

   • Am I often irritable? – If so, add 1 point

- Am I almost always irritable? – If so, add 2 points
(if the answer to both of these questions is yes, then your score so far is 3)

- Do I worry often? – If so, add 1 point

- When I worry, do I actually feel physically upset? – If so, add 2 points

- Do I think deeply about my problems? – If so, add no points—this is constructive.

- Does my thinking about my problems often block out my other thoughts? – If so, add 2 points

- Have I suffered panic attacks more than once in the last year? – If so, add 4 points; if more than three times, add 4 additional points for a total of 8

- Do I often believe specific people mean me harm, without objective evidence? – If so, add 2 points

- Do I often believe even strangers who don't know me mean me harm? – If so, add 2 points

- Am I incessantly worried about what people will say about me? – If so, add 2 points

- Do I frequently do or not do what I think is right just because I am worried what people will think – If so, add 2 points

- Do I avoid meeting new people or seeing people in general because I feel nervous around people? – If so, add 2 points

- Do I find it difficult to keep my mind on things I am trying to learn or do? – If so, add 2 points

- Do I fear leaving my home or other safe places, and find it uncomfortable to go out in the world? – If so, add 3 points

- Do I frequently use alcohol or other unprescribed drugs, or abuse prescribed medications in order to feel normal or happy? – If so, add 4 points

- Do I find myself repeatedly compulsively drawn to certain activities or thoughts, such as an obsession for being clean or thin, or being the life of the party or a know it all? – If so, add 2 points

- Do I cut my body or disfigure myself in other ways? – If so, add 4 points
- Do I try to constantly try to get sexual access to people and never feel satisfied? – If so, add 4 points

(Potential maximum score = 45)

If you scored 20 points or higher we believe that this could indicate severe anxieties. Don't worry, the Five Gates Program can help you substantially reduce this score. If you sense that your anxieties are interfering with your ability to take yourself through the Five Gates Training, you may want to go to the Five Gates and discuss this with a certified Five Gates Trainer.

If you scored above 15 and less than 20, we believe you are experiencing a high-level anxieties.

If you scored 10 but less than 15, we believe you are having significant levels of anxieties.

If you scored 5 but less than 10, our experiences shows that you have a fairly normal of anxieties and can benefit greatly by taking the Five Gates Program.

If you scored less than 5 points, your spiritual condition is very good for anxieties, but the Five Gates Program can help you achieve more. Many of our graduates with higher anxiety scores have reduced them to 0 and near 0.

2. *Do I have depression? Depression usually results from prolonged higher levels of anxiety. Once we have lost hope our anxieties will pass we tend to become depressed and feel hopeless.*

- Do I often feel as though I don't have the energy to move or get out of bed? – If so, add 3 points
- Do I have a sense or feeling "what's the use, nothing will go right for me no matter what I do?" – If so, add 5 points

- Do you feel lonely, but can't get yourself to go out in the world of people or go do things that you think you would probably enjoy if you could? – If so, add 5 points

- Does the world of colors often appear gray in my mind, with no known physiological cause? – If so, add 5 points

- Do I think about ending my life or wishing it would end? – If so, add 8 points and don't do it. The Five Gates Program will help you.

- Did I have one or more suicide attempts in the last 3 years? – If so, add 10 points if you were drinking or using drugs at the time; add 20 points if you were sober. This program can help you enjoy your life, so don't do it again.

- Do you frequently use alcohol or other unprescribed medications, or abuse prescribed medications in order to feel normal or happy, and they no longer work well? – If so, add 5 points

(Potential maximum score = 51)

If your total score was 10 points or higher, please consult with a physician and follow their directions. You may also want to possibly take the Five Gates Program preferably with a Five Gates Certified Trainer. Contact www.fivegates.com for more information.

If your score was 5 points or more but less than 10, the Five Gates Training can help you bring it down significantly, but you may also wish to consult a physician.

If your score was less than 5 but more than 0, you may be suffering from mild depression which you can most likely resolve by taking yourself through the Five Gates Program.

If your score was 0 or near 0, but you are suffering significant anxieties, intervention now will likely prevent you from becoming clinically depressed.

3. Do I have low self-esteem?

If your score for anxiety was lower than 5 you probably do not suffer from low self-esteem unless your depression score was above 0. Experience has shown us that higher anxiety and depression scores are always linked to low self-esteem.

- I believe my mother, father, brother, sister, spouse, or significant other does not love me. – add 0 points, since possibly they don't.
- I believe my mother, father, brother, sister, spouse, or significant other does not love me and this constantly troubles me. – add 5 points
- I find myself afraid to try to do things in which I fear I will fail. – add 5 points
- I feel a need to humiliate or make fun of other people or have them humiliate and make fun of me. – add 5 points
- When I meet people, I am ashamed to tell them things about myself or I can't seem to stop talking about my self and often exaggerate my virtues. – add 5 points
- I often get into ridiculous arguments or disagreements over things that don't matter just because I need to prove I'm smart. – add 5 points
- I often put other people down unnecessarily. – add 5 points
- I keep starting projects like school or jobs, but I never seem to stick to them to their conclusion. – add 5 points
- I seem to value clothes, cars, houses, and other material possessions much more than most. – add 5 points
- I feel ashamed about how I look or other things about myself when there seems to be no good reason for this. – add 5 points
- My pattern of life decisions and actions shows that I am unwilling to invest self-improvement. – add 5 points

- I'm loud, aggressive, or possibly sometimes offensive when there is no good purpose to this kind of behavior. – add 5 points
- I abuse weaker people and this makes me feel better. – add 5 points
- I am constantly judgmental of other people. – add 5 points
- I am constantly reliving the past instead of focusing in the present and what I need to do now. – add 5 points
- I constantly think I'm better than other people. – add 0 points if its true; and 10 points if it's not (don't score this one, just keep in mind that none of us are any better than anyone else. We may have achieved more, but we will soon see we are all a product of our lives and we can never know the path that another person's shoes have traveled.)

(Potential maximum score = 70)

If you believe or are troubled by the idea that people don't love you, this shows that you are not satisfied with the love you are able to give yourself. To that extent, you are suffering from low self-esteem.

If you find yourself afraid to try to do things or complete them because you have a fear of failure, you are suffering from low self-esteem.

If you often embarrass or make fun of people who are suffering from low self-esteem, you are suffering from low self-esteem.

If your score was 20 points or higher, we think you have a self-esteem problem. Our advise to you is to start working the program before it gets worse.

If your score was at least 10 but not as much as 20, you also have a self-esteem problem, but you can stop and eat your lunch if your hungry, and then start taking yourself through the Five Gates Training Program.

If your score was less than 10, you may want to retake this evaluation and then take yourself through the Five Gates

Program, since all of us seem to have more than this amount of self-doubt.

4. *Happiness Scale*

- I almost never feel happy. – add 5 points
- My moods go up and down more than I think other people's do. – add 3 points
- I feel like I never belong anywhere I am; if you are not living in a hospital, jail, or an insane asylum – add 5 points.
- I never seem to remember my happy experiences, but I keep focusing on my unhappy ones. – add 8 points
- I am always looking for reasons for why I won't have a good time instead of reasons I will. – add 5 points
- I always think the cup is half empty and not half full. – add 5 points, unless there is a whole in your cup
- I am never able to hold onto relationships, even when I want to. – add 5 points
- I hold onto relationships I don't want, but can't help myself. – add 8 points
- I am more than 40 years old since I was a child and have never lived for a year or longer with someone I loved. – add 5 points
- I know I am unhappy. – add 20 points
- I know I am happy. – you must be right.

Don't score this one; just ask yourself whether or not you are happy. If you're not sure, you're not happy, I promise you will be much happier after you take the Five Gates Training Program.

If you don't think you have any of these problems and you want a refund for the price of this book...forget it. Give it to a friend who needs it more.

PART THREE

IT'S TIME TO BEGIN OUR HEALING JOURNEY

THE FIRST GATE

Our Acknowledgement Of Our Problems

Statement of the First Gate:

"I have been powerless over something in me that causes me to believe, and therefore feel, to think and therefore act in ways that diminish my happiness."

The Purpose of the First Gate

The purpose of the First Gate is to help us focus our attention on the first important truth so that we can begin our journey. That important truth is that we are less happy than we want to be and, possibly, also doing destructive things such as taking drugs, gambling, or using other compulsive "fixes" to try to distract ourselves from our bad feelings. We may have a bad temper, or impulsively say hostile things. We may find ourselves to be unrealistically holding on to ideas or even lies that we can't agree with when we're honest with ourselves and others. We may have a dysfunctional relationship, or several of them. What our symptoms are is less important than our need to see them and accept that they are causes of unhappiness in our lives. As we work our way through the Five Gates Training Program, we'll see that these behaviors are all driven by our anxieties.

For those of us who only experience anxiety and possibly depression as our problems, we can visualize them as dysfunctional interferences with our happiness. We know that anxiety disorders and depression are often accompanied by neuro-chemical imbalances, but we also know that our psychological condition interacts with our neurochemistry so that the chemical problems may likely have been caused by the long-term or intense impact of the wrong views on which our personal psychology is based. One way to view anxiety and depression is that they are driven by our addiction to seeing ourselves and life in inaccurate perspectives. If our anxieties and depression is intense, it would be wise to seek the counsel of our physician to find out if a temporary mood stabilizer will help us work our program better. But even with this relief, only changing our visions of ourselves and the world can bring us the fullest happiness possible.

We see addictions of all kinds, including addictions to alcohol and other drugs, as problems in themselves, but we also see them as the symptoms of deeper problems which drive us to them compulsively for relief. Once we have removed the deeper problems, as we will do here, our craving for our addictions will diminish as well.

Some cravings are also believed by many experts to be organically driven and may require separate medical treatment. To my experience, the psychological aspects of cravings, once a good detox is taken, is by far more important and for most of my clients all they need. Experience shows that cravings will always diminish sharply with changes of our perspectives and time away from using our addictions.

We start by passing through this Gate, first, because this job is not about changing anything outside ourselves. Our focus is to identify something in ourselves that is diminishing our happiness, and to do this we use our feelings. Our feelings are the surest indicators of our spiritual condition.

The First Gate Statement reads: "I have been powerless over something in me that causes me to believe, and therefore feel, to think, and, therefore, act in ways that diminish my happiness."

Let's examine what this means.

- *"I have been..."* We say that we have been powerless in this way because we don't know the future, but we hope for the better. We know that to some degree, this statement will be true at times of stress or misunderstandings. Because this is so, we will always be able to make the declaration of our First Gate as a statement of truth, for as long as we're human beings, therefore imperfect in our faith and our knowledge, and, therefore, in our ability to live happily.

- "…*powerless.…*" We say we are powerless because it has been a long time since we were doing or believing things that were wrong, thinking things that didn't seem to make sense, or feeling awful, often without even knowing why. Even when we thought we knew why, we were probably wrong anyway. We found we couldn't stop doing and thinking these things, and yet we found ourselves unable to stop. By powerlessness, we mean there's a part of us that doesn't agree with what we at times were believing, thinking, feeling and doing, but we've been unable to stop these things from running our lives, causing our suffering and most importantly, interfering with our happiness.

- "…*something in me.…*" This is the first key to unlocking the doors of our real prison. Self-knowledge is the first key to our freedom from all our suffering. The world has many ways to frustrate our best intentions and efforts, but the only power we will ever have is the power to manage ourselves as best we can in the present. Therefore, our challenge always lies within us. But, at first this isn't always easy to see, and even harder to accept.

- "…*believe and therefore feel…*" We know from science that lower animals have feelings, but, believe it or not, many animals can lose a limb and not grieve or suffer, even if they do feel pain. Suffering is caused by our belief that something is happening, or has happened, which should not have. Our deepest suffering is the result of our believing we will not be able to fix the problem it has caused in us. It is our judgmental beliefs, not what is going on or even our pain, that causes us suffering. If we can change what we see and believe, we can change our feelings naturally. For those of us who are addicts, we used to try to do this with "using," and when we stopped using, but had not solved the problems of our deepest beliefs, we still craved using to escape the negative feelings they caused in us.

• *"….think and therefore do…"* Our beliefs and senses feed us the information on which we base our thoughts and decisions to act. In our First Gate we focus on our thoughts and the actions they cause us to take. Our beliefs, the platform on which are thoughts operate, are the targets in our efforts to change ourselves, including what we do.

• *"…diminished my happiness…"* If you were satisfied with your happiness now, you wouldn't want to change anything about yourself, except possibly getting more physically fit or learning more about subjects important to your enjoyment or accomplishment of your goals.

There may be a part of us that wants to disown the fact that we are always doing what we think is the right thing at all times. There is a part of us that may be saying, "This is crazy. It's not the right thing to do, but I keep doing it." That means that there is also a more deeply buried irrational part of ourselves that makes the decision that this is the right thing to do regardless of the conflict and consequences that result from it. These parts can be very irrational and nonsensical, especially at our times of greatest vulnerability and weakness. We must never forget that the goal of our recovery program is happiness and health. Others may have wanted us to work the recovery program because they thought we should stop using drugs, stop gambling, stop our compulsive spending or compulsive eating, stop arguing or getting arrested, stop being anxiety-ridden and having panic attacks or being depressed. Chances are those people just want to control our behavior to make life more convenient for themselves. They don't really see that being able to put down all these other forms of destructive behavior lies in our finding a way to be happy and at peace with ourselves.

Our First Gate acts like a beacon for us. It shows us where to go. It helps us see our real problems. It remains with us throughout all of our lives, no matter how well we get or how we may at times experience setbacks or suffering. By keeping this First Gate acknowledgment there, we can always reground ourselves in a clear, comprehensive, truthful and accurate statement of what it is that lies at the root of our problems.

We focus on the issue of our happiness, not whether or not we take drugs, get good grades in school, make top salesman in our job or are the best athlete on the field. We know from experience that happy people are generous, loving and well loved by all who know them, if their happiness is real and they share it in the way we teach in the Five Gates Training Program. This kind of happiness multiplies itself throughout all aspects of our lives, just as our unhappiness imprisoned us.

How to See Our Need for Personal Redevelopment?

We always crave to cling to being self-sufficient. Only someone who knows they are a suffering prisoner of their anxieties, depressions and addictions can glibly say: "I've been powerless over something in *me*, which has caused me to *believe*, and therefore *feel*, *think*, and therefore *do* things that have taken away my happiness."

In our First Gate, we identify that our problems, the ones we can really do anything about, are in us. We come to this conclusion through the following insights:

1. If we know we can't do something, it's no use for us to believe that we can do it. Believing that we must be or do what we believe we can't be or do does not help us do anything at all, and harms us by making us feel inadequate. Our first wisdom is we must accept our proven limitations without judging ourselves inadequate because of them.

2. We can influence the world, but we can manage only ourselves and only that to the best of our abilities at that time. Even our efforts to influence the world are part of managing ourselves. The acceptance of the limitations in all of us is essential to start our journey through the First Gate.

3. If we cling to the idea that all our main problems are in the world outside of us, we can't make the great commitment needed to improve ourselves, or even be active in changing our world, since we can only try to do that by managing ourselves better.

4. The harsh winds or pleasant breezes of my physical environment will cause me to have feelings, but all of the other factors in my feelings are responses to how I see my reality.

5. I accept that aside from the physical environment, what I believe is the cause of my feelings.

6. My feelings are a fact, and real. When we combine the information of my feelings with my understandings of cause and effect, the result is my decision to act in whatever way I do. Even my thoughts are actions within me since they influence my feelings and everything I do.

7. The present is the result of all the past. If I don't like what's going on within me now, I must find the logical causes in me and work toward changing them. This includes the part my physical nature plays in causing my limitations. I must focus on the problems in me.

8. I must accept that everything I can't do I shouldn't do. The only thing I can do is to try to manage myself better.

We can overcome our natural resistance to accepting our need for change by seeing that changing ourselves is the greatest form of self-empowerment.

Why I Needed to See the First Gate's Truth — The Solutions Are in Me

It's not really necessary, at first, to know very much about what has caused us to feel anxieties, depressions or have compulsive behavior such as addictions to alcohol and other drugs. Other possible symptoms are our inability to function or focus for more than a few moments. This is called attention-deficit disorder (ADD). Some of us may have experienced a compulsion to abuse alcohol and drugs, disfigure our bodies, gamble, be violent, pursue meaningless sexual activity, abuse food or starve ourselves, abuse exercise, work or any of a wide variety of possible symptoms. All of these are driven by our anxieties and depressions.

We know this because Five Gates graduates overcome all of these problems because they are strongly motivated. We see that the "something" that causes all of this is not about the world around us, but about something inside us. For as long as we continue to insist that our problems are primarily owing to the world around us, and that our solution will come from changes in the world around us, we can make no progress in our recovery.

We have learned that underneath our anxieties and depressions are two primary causes. One potential cause is the chemistry of our brains. Depressive or anxiety-fragile brain chemistry can be brought about by long-term fear, driven by wrong ideas about who we are. Sometimes, these wrong ideas are hard to find as our causes of anxiety. We are too easily tempted to believe the possibility that we may have inherited these tendencies from our original organic nature. But, it doesn't really matter which one is the cause, since we only have one business in this matter, and that is to address this problem now.

The answer is two-fold. We must try to restore the chemical balance of our brain system. Removing unprescribed drugs and other interfering factors that physically impact our neurological condition can help do this. We may also make some improvements by taking medications designed for this purpose. These are called psychotropic medications, and they are obtained through a visit to a psychiatrist. This person will do an analysis and ultimately prescribe medication, if medication is needed. But medication will not be enough. The fact is that we must learn a way of thinking, a way of seeing ourselves that gives us courage, joy and productive activity of our minds, behavior, feelings and thoughts. That is the goal of our recovery program.

A chemical imbalance in our brain chemistry will not cause us to think specific ideas, but will rather make us more vulnerable to holding onto negative ideas that we would have otherwise dismissed, or put into perspective. Therefore, if we can learn a way of thinking that perpetually restores our positive perspective, this method will address our anxieties and our depressions whether their sources are organic, became organic or are entirely psychological.

We conclude, therefore, that although there may be many things about the world we would like to see changed, our mission in recovery is solely to change ourselves. The change required is to address that something in us that has caused us to believe and therefore feel, think and do things that have decreased our happiness.

The purpose of the First Gate is to help us focus our attention on this first important truth--we need to accept that the problem and the solution to our condition lies within us in order to begin our journey to wellness. We start by passing through this Gate first because, without it, we have no motivation that will cause us to want to change the things we must change so that we can have a happy and productive life. This job won't do itself, and it is not about changing anything outside of us. Unlike the traditional 12-step program of A.A, our focus is on identifying that our repairable difficulty is in us and not that we are powerless over alcohol or anything outside us. It may well be that our lives have sunken into some degree of ruin. This doesn't matter, because if you work your way through the acceptance and understanding of the realizations you will find here, your life can become joyful, productive and free of suffering.

My First Gate Share

I was always a control freak. But before I got into my most depressive years, the ones in which I was a hard-core alcoholic, I had been able to wander in life. I tried one thing after another, letting go whenever the path seemed too easy, too difficult, less interesting than when I started, or when what I was doing was sure to fail. Many times, I let go of what I was doing and turned my attention to starting a new adventure. I made up some rationalization about why I wanted the change.

One day, I got myself into a marriage and a business. This was something from which I could not run when things got tough. My marriage was based on my business aspirations and my business aspirations were based on my ego needs. I had a failing marriage that I couldn't get out of in one piece, as I saw it, unless I first succeeded at what I was doing. My wife's and my total fortunes and ego were all tied up in this business. I was buying and redeveloping real estate during the same years that almost everyone in the business went broke.

The control freak in me said I had to be able to control the people and circumstances of my life, or finally accept that I was a loser. Somehow, I lost my ability to put anything into perspective except my increasingly desperate need to get the power and money, both of which I needed to feel okay about myself. I accepted this belief without questioning until it nearly killed me. As my struggles and losses became greater, I kept focusing on the world outside myself, trying to find ways to make it do what I wanted it to do. When my world started sliding backwards, I tried even more desperate tactics to try to win my struggle. Every aspect of my life was distorted by my sense of desperation. I had nowhere to turn, and only fought harder.

When this didn't work, I started to drink alcohol to escape my anxieties and depression. Instead of starting out in a new direction and trying to find another way to be happy, I just drank more and more, until finally I collapsed. I sensed there was a problem in me, but I thought I could fix that after I won my struggle with the world. It didn't work, and later, when I found another path to feel good about myself, I was able to write the First Gate in order to remind myself that anytime I ever feel anxiety-ridden or depressed again, I must look for the source of my problem in me. This is what I needed to learn and accept from the wisdom of the First Gate.

How Do We Know We Have Successfully Completed the First Gate?

All we need from the First Gate is to accept the truth that the problems that reduced our feelings of well being are inside of us. We must see the connections between our beliefs as they drive our feelings and thoughts, and how, together, they all determine our choices for actions. To the extent we see and accept this, we have taken the First Gate successfully. Just the fact that we are making progress in our understanding of how we work will possibly raise your spirits and give you added enthusiasm. We want to break free of the idea that the world outside us is where our problems lie. Later, we will see and understand this truth better. If you find this idea still impossible to accept, we recommend that you spend some more time thinking about it and reviewing the First Gate.

THE SECOND GATE

Discovery of the Sources of Our Problems

Statement of the Second Gate:

"That something in me is my incorrect beliefs and the fears they bring upon me. I don't want to allow them to run my life anymore."

In the First Gate we accepted that something in us was the cause of our problem thoughts and actions. Now we're ready to examine what that something is.

- *"That something in me..."* The generator of the wrong ideas and troubled feelings in me.

- *"...are my incorrect beliefs..."* What I don't know that I need to know in my heart to rid myself of my dysfunctional beliefs, which cause my troubled feelings, distorted thinking, and foolish actions.

- *"...and the fears they bring upon me..."* We accept that to have a peaceful positive mind, heart, and positive actions we must be free of our irrational fears.

- *"...I don't want to allow them to run my life anymore!"* We accept that there is a connection between our problems and our fears, which drive our troubled thoughts and feelings and our actions. We commit ourselves to correcting our beliefs and seeking our enlightenment.

Why I Needed to See the Truth of the Second Gate

My Second Gate Share

I was afraid that if I lost my money and had to face the shame of bankruptcy and having lost all of my wife's money, I couldn't bear it. Desperately, I started cutting corners, drinking more heavily and lying to myself to the point that I didn't even know what was true anymore. I started looking for affirmations from strange women, picking fights and arguments I was sure I could win, became a slick, self-righteous bully, while all the while I lied to my wife, not telling her that the bills I paid each month were getting older and older, and the ones I couldn't pay were piling higher and higher. As I became this person I hated, I started looking like him too. I had a sallow complexion with a puffy, greasy face, red eyes and a bulging stomach. In my depression, I was barely able to move my body with any grace at all, even though I had once been an athlete. I threatened people to get what I wanted from them, and exploited their fears and vulnerabilities to get my way. My whole outlook on life was distorted by my fear and "the children of my fear": lies, abuse, self-destructiveness, drunkenness, anxiety and depression so deep that even in the Florida mid-day sun, the world I saw was dark and gloomy. I didn't know it was possible for me to stop these fears from running my life. It took the wisdom of the Five Gates Training Program to show me how to live a more positive life based on humility, love and hope.

Purpose and Truth of the Second Gate

In the First Gate, we accepted that something inside ourselves has been causing us to believe, feel, think and do things that take away our happiness. In the Second Gate, we identify that "something" to be our fears, ignorance and mistaken beliefs, and label all of them as "children of fear," even though the wrong ideas we were taught brought our fears upon us. It's not enough for you just to see the idea of these connections. You will need to identify some examples of how your fears and ignorance have distorted your beliefs and ideas, and caused your anxieties and possibly depression to drive your self-destructive actions. We don't need to try to see all of this when we take our Second Gate, because we can't. Much more of that truth is revealed in our Fourth and Fifth Gates. For now, do you see that we have been misguided in some ways that caused us bad feelings and unwise choices?

Our Journey through the Second Gate

The statement of the Second Gate is best understood when it is read as a continuation of the First Gate: "I have been powerless over something in me that causes me to believe and therefore feel, to think and therefore act in ways that diminish my happiness," followed by, "That 'something' is my incorrect beliefs and the fears they bring upon me, and I don't want to allow them to run my life anymore!" Taken together as one idea the First and Second Gates say "I have been powerless over my fears and ignorance, which have diminished my happiness, and I don't want to run my life anymore." Here, once again, we are focusing in on our real problem, that is our fears and ignorance are spoiling our lives

In the Five Gates Program we believe that ignorance and wrong ideas are the cause of our useless and often destructive fears. Ignorance isn't just something that causes us not to buy the right stock, know the right thing to say, or memorize the answers to a school test. Ignorance, in this case, focuses on the errors that we make that lead us into unproductive fears. Let's stop and take a look.

What is a productive fear and what is an unproductive fear? If a baseball is whizzing toward my head, and I can see it, there may be time to duck if I have sufficient coordination and enough adrenalin in my bloodstream to let me get out of the way quickly. In that case, the fear that generates the adrenalin in me would be a productive fear. This situation doesn't come up much, though. I think we want to believe our fears are necessary to protect us against harm, but most of the time, they are not at all productive, and those of us who suffer from anxiety and depression, they are destructive. The question is how do we rid ourselves of unproductive fears?

To rid ourselves of distracting unproductive fears, we focus on the fact that we can only have one job in life, to do our best to do the next right thing. Everything else we think we can do is either a lie taught to us in our co-dependent childhoods and then carried into our adulthoods, or part of a mistaken over-expansion of our ego. We can't change the past and we can't know the future. We can guess at the likely outcomes based on our previous experience, but everything we have the power to do we can only do in the present. The only thing we *can* do in the present is to try our best to know, do, enjoy and learn from finding the next right thing. As human beings, that's all we were given to work with and, therefore, it does us no good to believe that we need any other power than that. This means that every kind of fear that does not help us do the next right thing is not only completely unproductive, but also it's actually destructive, as witnessed by the fact that if we look at the reasons we suffer from anxiety and depression, it is because we have fears that are not yet answered. We have fears that consume us with pointless worry. When we are anxiety-ridden or depressed, we can't see our way around them. We can't allay them sufficiently so we could go on doing the only thing we can do, managing ourselves to our best ability in the present.

All our unproductive fears diminish us. Can you see this is 99 percent of our fears? Our fears bring us down, rob us of our joy and efficiency, prevent us from focusing on the next right thing to do to the best of our ability and diminish us in many ways. We want to rid ourselves of our unproductive fears, the ones that don't do any useful work, but what does this have to do with ignorance?

Some people actually feel safer being scared. They mistake fear for caution in hopes that being afraid will protect them. I know this sounds pretty crazy, but sometimes people, as a matter of learned behavior, have come to believe that being scared is actually helpful in keeping them safe and productive.

When this happens, we have confused the positive benefits of caution with the destructive harm of our irrational fears. Our failure to know the difference between useful caution and unproductive fear comes from our ignorance. But, we did not invent this ignorance. We were taught or shown that we should think this way while we were growing up. Let's look at this in more detail. It's an unfortunate belief system that would lead us to a place like this, and this is something, if it's true of us, we very much need to see. Few friends will be won by the man who tells them that if the ride on the roller coaster feels great, they've got a problem, that they're craving fear as a form of stimulation because we have become overly dulled to the normal joys and sensual involvement with living.

This condition is almost invariably the result of depression to some degree. Work this program and that depression will leave you. Continue to live this program and that depression will not only not come back, but your sensual involvement, your joy in meeting each moment of life will be so increased you won't miss the artificial methods, and all the different kinds of drugs we have used to stimulate ourselves into believing we were alive when it was our depression that was making us feel dead inside.

The reason our fears are caused by our ignorance is because some part of us has not fully accepted that unproductive fears are destructive and unnecessary. We have no ability to control the outcome of anything. If we can focus ourselves on that truth, we will suddenly feel our fears diminishing exactly in proportion to our ability to keep focusing on the next right thing to do. This is enlightened living, learning from these next rights things, enjoying them and, of course, trying to decide what they are by using our wisdom. In our next Gate, we will address the concept of surrender and wisdom.

Our ignorance and misguided ideas are usually caused not by anything we have done, or errors we have made, but are rather brought to us by the environment in which we matured, through our infancy and early childhood and sometimes our later childhood and adolescence. We may have been taught positive or negative views about our world. For example, "Our nurturing may have not included ideas like, "This world is a friendly place for those who will be friendly within it," "All we must do to have a good life is to find a positive way to serve ourselves and our fellow man," ideas such as "Bring all the trust you can afford to give and your world will trust you," or "Be a loving person and you will experience a loving world around you." Instead we may have been taught "Everyone is out to get you,""Winners grab everything they can and let everybody else worry about themselves," "You will never amount to much," "Your a born loser," or any of a number of fear-producing and negative ideas. Through our thoughts and actions we tend to create around us the world we were taught to see. Another way of saying this is "Our world is a mirror of us (Recover With Me, copyright 1998, Lynn Kesselman, Recovery Press)." There are many ideas we can learn in our childhoods that will give us a positive and productive attitude about life, without making us unreasonably vulnerable to naïve, destructive expectations. We must come to accept our mortality and fragility, accept them as who we are. It is not something that's wrong, but something to be addressed with the best of our abilities. Surely, one day we will all become infirm unless we die suddenly. Surely, the world is a place of energies, hazards and other things that can bring our injury or death, but that does not mean we should not walk forward in life to seek pleasure, adventure and a meaningful life of service.

To the extent that our early life has failed to teach us the positive views, we may be operating with ideas that have caused us to behave foolishly or destructively, we must unlearn those ideas. We must learn to reject them. We must reach into our deepest, inner core and not only reject our wrong ideas, but replace them with ideas that are more functional, more positive and more productive towards giving us a good life. The secret of how to do this lies later in the Five Gates Training Program. We will learn methods by which we can actually change our deepest, inner beliefs. All we need to accept for now is that it is our ignorance and our mistaken beliefs are the causes of our fears which result in our negative feelings, thoughts and actions that have diminished our happiness.

How Can I Know If I Have Successfully Journeyed through the Second Gate?

Prior to taking our Fourth and Fifth Gates, we can only understand and accept our Second Gate in part. Our minds are turning inwardly to try to see examples of how our beliefs have been driving our negative feelings, and how our actions have often not made logical sense to us. Possibly, they have been self-destructive. For now, we have completed our journey through the Second Gate. After we have taken our Fourth and Fifth Gates, we will understand the truth of the Second Gate's role in our lives with much greater clarity.

THE THIRD GATE

We Commit to Changing Ourselves By Changing How We Think and What We Do

Statement of the Third Gate:

"I want to learn, accept and practice living by the positive principles that work best in my reality as it really is, not the negative ones inspired by my fears."

- *"I want to learn to accept..."* It's not enough to be told what is true, even if that truth can save our lives or restore our peace of mind. We need to find a way that we will not only see, but will also at our deepest levels, help us believe the important truths that will heal us.

- *"...learn to practice..."* It's not enough for us to believe the truths that will heal us. We must learn through practice and meditation (directed thinking) the many different ways we can best apply our new wisdom to the management of our lives.

- *"...living by positive principles that work best in my reality as it really is..."* We start with some common sense reality rules which we believe accurately describe how we work in the world. Over time we refine and expand them in accordance with our experience as we try our best to apply them in our daily lives.

- *"...not the negative ones inspired by my fears."* Through the study of our lives, we discover that our compulsive and destructive choices stemmed directly from our fear-ridden perspectives.

Purpose and Truth of the Third Gate: We Want To Learn How to Live Positively Without Our Fears

The purpose of your Third Gate is to help you see and accept that you can manage your life more successfully by positive principles of thought and action and more accurate reality rules. We define the principles and reality rules which we wish to follow as the ones that will give us a happier and more productive life. As you read these pages, you will probably wonder if you really could live by the principles you are about to see. If you try to do this right now, you would probably not be able to live by positive principles nearly as well as once you have completed your Fifth Gate. Do not spend a great time studying and reviewing the Third Gate since everything that appears here, and much more, will be in the first part of the Life Practice. At that time, your fears will be greatly dissolved and you will need these principles in order to replace your old fear-driven perspectives.

A good way to understand the Third Gate is to accept it in the same way we would the advice of our athletic coach who will try to teach us the best form we can use to maximize our athletic performance. In this case we are trying to learn how to maximize the way we process reality and the actions we take as the result of our understandings. Temporarily, this book will serve as your coach. But in your Life Practice you will increasingly take on that job for yourself and become your own coach.

Some Five Gate graduates have said that they could have gone from the end of the Second Gate, when they were able to accept that their problems were driven by their fears, right to the Fourth and Fifth Gates in order to prepare themselves to be better able to understand and follow the direction of the Third Gate. On the other hand, some Five Gates graduates have said they need this section in order to convince themselves that there really is an achievable and scientific method by which they can manage their lives for greater happiness.

The choice to stop for the Third Gate or to continue straight through to the Fourth Gate must be made by you, since only you know if you are ready to continue the strenuous task of being introspective about your life and your problem feelings. If you do go straight to the Fourth Gate and find that you lack the motivation to complete it thoroughly, come back and review the First Gate; you need to accept that the only problems you can solve are within you. After reviewing the First Gate, go to the Second Gate to see that your problems are tied to your fears and have been running your life. Then you may want to come back here to the Third Gate and see the scientific way we redirect our thoughts, feelings and actions in our new more positive way of life.

The Third Gate is the center focus of our Life Practice, but we cannot fully appreciate its power or use its tools effectively until we have completed our Fifth Gate. Remember, the primary goal of our Core Training, the first Five Gates, is to achieve the enlightenment-driven spiritual awakening which results from the completion of our Fifth Gate. We want to do this as soon as possible!

If you managed your life by the principles presented here, you could not be depressed or confused, only puzzled. You would not be emotionally addicted to anything, even though it may take some time living by these principles to eventually dissolve the hold that our ingrained patterns and habits still have over you. Later, you will learn that Five Gates graduates have reoccurrences of use, but rarely if ever have relapses. A relapse is a condition in which our progress towards wellness appears to have been lost because of a great disturbance which caused us to go back to thinking and acting in our old pre-recovery ways. A reoccurrence of use is only a misjudgment of the moment, which we will tend to correct quickly. We learn that we are finally courageous, and enlightened enough to see ourselves. The following are the key principles that drive our courage and enlightenment in the Five Gates Life Training Program. You may discover more!

Remember, you are your own trainer, even your own therapist, as you take yourself through this program. Don't be afraid to be creative, and especially repetitive. It is perfectly okay to gloat a little as you feel the progress of your new enlightenments channeling their way through you. If this makes you want to review the Third Gate again before you go onto the Fourth Gate, by all means do so. Just remember, though, you can't complain about the facilitator because that's you. In this Gate we present a number of recommended positive principles and reality rules. If any of them do not make sense to you or if you have additional ones that you wish to use, please change them so they look right to you. The first time through the Third Gate you will not want to invest too much effort into revising this list, but later after you have taken your Fifth Gate and especially as you gain experience in the Life Practice following the Fifth Gate you will continuously reexamine these principles and reality rules to see if they fit in your life experience.

Why I Needed to Learn the Truth of the Third Gate

My life had to crash and burn before I could begin to realize that it was possible to manage my life entirely by positive principles. I went broke and my wife divorced me. All my lifelong friends abandoned me and I had to come to dingy rooms, where others like me were telling their stories and trying to work their steps for regaining their lives. I started with no clue, except that I couldn't go on like I was previously. Actually, because of the condition I was in, I didn't have that option even if I'd wanted it. As I sat there, watching and listening, I came to see that what they were saying was true. The happiest of them seemed to live by positive principles, and after thinking about it for awhile I came to see that all the happy people I had ever known were living by just enough positive principles to help them love themselves. I figured that this was the secret to loving my life, too.

Each time I conscientiously faced a new situation, I found that loving spirit in me, the good character that gradually emerged from putting effort in this positive direction. It was bearing the most delicious fruit. I found I was becoming someone I really loved to be. I was still broke, but not broken anymore. And, without judging them or myself, everyone was my friend, even the ones who had not yet learned the value of living by positive principles for themselves.

Introduction To The Third Gate

All of us make many errors in the way we process reality; the world has taught us to make them in order that we will accept other people's views and agendas. Some examples of this inaccurate thinking are as follows.

- I will feel better about my situation if I can find that someone else is to blame instead of just figuring out how to do the next right thing to help myself.

- I am not connected to everyone and everything, but instead I am a world isolated to myself. We usually have this problem most severely when we are living in a state of fear.

- I will profit best if I focus only on getting what I immediately want for myself instead of balancing this with service for others.

- What other people believe about me is just as important or more important than what I believe about myself.

- I would be happy if I had more material possessions and more money. Please don't take this to mean that we can't live a more convenient life by having this security and convenience that money can buy, but my rich and poor clients suffer from exactly the same problems.

- There's no use to trying to work a program that claims it can change me because my neurochemistry is unchangeable. Research is increasingly revealing that the claims made for the Five Gates Program are potentially capable of changing our neurochemistry and not only our behavior.

- If I think about the past enough, I can change it and not just accept and work with its results in the present.

- I can accurately predict the outcomes of my actions and therefore I can control my world. We have found that it is a hard job just to manage our thoughts and actions, and that this is all we can actually do. Wisdom will help us predict their outcomes but can never control them.

- We mistake forgiveness with amnesia thinking that we want those who forgive us to forget things ever happened. To forgive is to understand and to accept that what happened was the natural consequence of forces acting at that moment in time, but not necessarily to be repeated.

- We think we know what we or other people should have done, instead of accepting that everyone is always doing the best they can and what they know at the time. When we accept this insight we stop judging people and see the truth of how much alike we all are except for experience that shaped us.

- We refuse to accept that what goes around comes around as applying centrally to our own attitudes and actions.

- We foolishly believe that our goal and how we judge ourself is by the standard of perfection when the truth is that the best we can do is keep improving.

- Our natural processes tell us that the future can be predicted by understanding the past. Even though this is too a large measure true, the problem it creates in us is that we travel through life believing that we are our history and not our possibilities. This form of self-judgment is one of the crippling causes of anxieties and depression and the resulting low-esteem they bring upon us.

- During our childhood which are our most co-dependent years, we blindly accept that some things are our job because we are told that they are, even if we can't do them. This causes us great anxieties which tend to live within us throughout our lives. In the Five Gates Program we correct this problem by accepting if we cannot do something it cannot be our job.

We can correct these and many other fallacies in our thinking by trying our best and constantly improving our ability to manage our lives by the Five Gates positive principles and reality rules which follow. You may think of some we have overlooked. At the end of our list we will give you examples of some special personal rules you might want to create for yourself. Each person is different with respect to the ones on which they need to focus most.

The Reality Rules and Principles of Our Third Gate

In our program we tend to use the term "reality rule" to mean a statement which is provable on simple terms. An example of this is, "We can not change the past." A principle is a way of looking at things or behaving that experience has proven to be wise and good for us. An example of this is, "My world is a mirror of me," which means what I put out will come back to me in the longer run. Many people will have their own ways of expressing these and others not included here. The key point is that we must learn to manage ourselves in accordance with reality rules and positive we have accepted as truth.

REALITY RULES

- If I cannot do something, it cannot be my job. As logical and clear as this principle is, it's amazing how many people go through life accepting that other people can reasonably hold them responsible for doing what they cannot do. This battle causes anxiety, and until we find the hope that removes that anxiety, we are very vulnerable to depression. Psychological depression is the result of anxieties that are unrelieved and have no hope of being relieved.

- I cannot change the past, therefore I must never believe that changing the past could possibly be my job, or even that it would be a desirable thing to do. When we accept this principle, we also must accept the idea that the past is perfect. We have no way to know that anything was ever any different than it should have been, and because we cannot change it, the most positive belief we can adopt is that the past was perfect in every way.

- The present is also perfect. Here's where we may get into some trouble. If we say the present is perfect, why would we ever want to bring about change? For that matter, why would we want to do anything? The present is nothing more than the inevitable, logical and completely certain result of the past, and since we cannot change the present any more than we can change the past, we must accept that it is perfect as being the present, but not perfect for being the future. The future is the time in which anything will be different than it is at this particular moment. In the present, our only job is to act in ways that will bring about a future we desire to the best of our ability.

- My only job in life is to manage me to the best of my ability. Is there any other job that we could possibly do? Of course not since we cannot make anyone else's finger move or cause anyone else to think our thoughts. Our only power with respect to other people is to influence them through whatever methods may be available to us through managing ourselves in the present. Could we manage ourselves in the past? We have, and that part is unchangeable. However, we can change our futures by living these principles in the present.

- Everything was, is and always will be exactly as it should be. This is an extension of earlier principles, but brings upon us the therapeutic benefit of peace. We do not wish to be passive with respect to those things we can do, those that relate to managing our actions, our attitudes and our feelings in the present. But with respect to everything else, we want to be completely passive. This is because we don't want to give any space, room or energy to that which we cannot help. In seeing this, we rescue ourselves from so many forms of insanity, illness, and disease in our lives.

- We accept that we have no power over anything or anyone whatsoever, except limited control over our own behavior and thoughts. Through our actions we may conditionally have *influence* on the world around us, the kind of influence is the point. This rule tells us that we cannot know or have control over any outcomes. Our failure to accept this and forgive ourselves for our limitations is much of what led us to ruin. We need humility and acceptance to change that.

- We accept that it does us no good to preoccupy ourselves with what others think or do, except where our constructive concern will teach us something useful and cause us to perform an action that will serve a useful purpose. Otherwise, it's none of our business. Our codependency is a symptom of our not seeing this and not accepting it. Too often, we chase after people's praise or acceptance instead of just trying to do the next right thing. Once again we seek calm, loving, grateful acceptance of life as it is.

- Nothing happens by mistake or outside of the rules of reality; we are constantly learning those rules so we won't be surprised or need to be superstitious.

PRINCIPLES

- My world acts as a mirror to me. By this we mean that if we put positive actions, feelings and ideas into the world around us, we will perceive a more positive world for ourselves.

- When we smile at the people around us, we receive smiles back. When we grimace, complain, lie or are deceitful, if we are violent, dishonest or in any other way negative, our world will become more negative, not only because of our view of ourselves, but because the world will not welcome us in a positive, loving manner.

- I will never do anything perfectly except be me. What this means is that no one is perfect. All of us overlook truths, all of us react out of fears, and all of us put out a negative signal because of our fears, anxieties or misunderstandings. Our errors are in our failure to improve our understanding and our inability to perform positive acts. This principle really says I must judge no one as being different than they should be, not even myself.

- Many things are our business that aren't our fault. Fault is a judgmental concept and has no place in sane living, personal development or happiness. Everything we do comes about as a result of influences acting upon us and others, so nothing is really our fault. But trying to fix what's "broken" is our business.

- We accept that it does us no good, in fact it does us harm to resent anything at all. Resentment wastes our emotional energies and may cause us to take foolish actions. Resentment is always an expensive drug leading us away from constructive actions. "Resentment is the poison we drink foolishly believing it will harm the other guy (Golis)."

- We accept the world as it is without complaining about it, unless our complaint is a useful part of a constructive, realistic effort to bring about positive changes. Complaining by itself does no one any good, and in most situations it can bring harm. When we complain without useful purpose, we're refusing to accept truth.

- We accept that our constructive intentions are not good enough to justify our ever taking needless destructive actions. To bring good without harm to anyone is good but not always possible. We must be very careful not to play God. Breaking good principles for what we believe are good motives is dangerous because we are flawed and we might be tempted to break them for self-serving reasons. Our motives are key, but we should distrust any behavior that violates positive (loving) principles. We must approach this subject with great caution and seek the advice of the wise and loving.

- We accept that we can consciously do only one thing at a time, the next thing we think or do. Of course, we are capable of multi-tasking, but we're made to be able to consciously focus on only one thing at a time. We must train ourselves to calm down, step back, and make constructive plans and decisions. This is meditation. We must not expect particular results, but rather accept what happens as what is right for now, and make new plans when the old ones are no longer useful. We must adjust realistically to our abilities and choices, and not fight reality.

- We accept that whenever we are upset, we are fearful about something. Few fears are useful in directing or helping us to lovingly and gratefully do the next right thing.

- We accept that we must try to do each next thing exactly in accordance with loving motives and behavior principles. We must try to perform acts of kindness and service for others and ourselves and try not to bring harm. By this principle we add the element of our support to all those around us. When we help others we are usually wise not to worry what's in us for us. We will find the world is good to those who are generous.

- Everyone always did, is doing and always will do the best they can at managing themselves. It does us no good to believe anything else is true. People are not intentionally trying to do less than their best. That is their best, to be doing what they'd like to be doing, what they find important, what they find valuable, what they find possible and what they understand will bring about the results they desire.

- I must strive to see the ways in which I am exactly like everyone else. The purpose of this principle is to try to help us overcome the lies that society invariably teaches us. All social activity focuses us on the differences between people rather than their sameness. To grasshoppers, we all look pretty much alike, have about the same amount of intelligence and probably smell equally as bad. The fact is that by seeing ourselves as similar, we can feel one another's pain and celebrate each other's joy. The result is a sense of comfort and an inspiration for higher morality, generosity and love. It also brings a sense of community and purpose.

We must try to learn to trust in the fact that the results of accepting these rules will be good for us. We can only see that they are good by giving them a fair and patient try. For some of us, the bad news is that none of us seem to have very much power over anything. The good news is that we now have some simple, rational methods by which we can live life without ego-driven fears. We don't have to worry about anything when it is not our job. Worry is the opposite of joy. We don't ever benefit from worry! Good planning and caution are useful.

Spirituality-Producing (Reality-Accepting) Reminders

- I must seek and not resist truth and wisdom. They are my best friends.
- My only job in life is to manage myself as well as I can right now, and avoid needless competition with everything in life, even myself.
- I can't manage my life well without following positive, loving principles, even when they're inconvenient, seem unfair, frighten me, or lead me to help those who despise me.
- Everyone's joy and pain touches me, and mine touches them.
- My being of loving service to myself and others is almost always the same thing, even helping those who oppose or misunderstand me!
- Everything that's true now is the result of the past.

- We have always done the best we could.

- My bad feelings are *mine*, and are not about the world around me.

- We are too often deceived into thinking of love as barter, not as an inspiration summoning a reciprocal desire to give. The greatest gift we give to anyone is to help a person love himself.

- "No man is an island." Our fears cause us to have too much faith in fences, and not enough in love. Give to those in pain, especially to those who may seem unworthy. Just be careful that the gift is motivated by loving concern, and not a payoff for unloving behavior.

- Life will inevitably bring us pain at times. Some pain is useful in helping us make good decisions, but suffering may reflect our error of judgment in believing that we know better than what reality has brought to us. Our resentments come from a combination of our fears and desire to control creation. This leads us to reject our limitations, and from this we fall into the trap of depressions. Depression is caused when we believe we must do what we believe we cannot. The result is a perpetual fear response. This can even alter our brain chemistry. Accepting spiritual principles can give us the peace to reverse this destructive process.

Our Morality

Our loving behavior is an essential part of our getting well. Our knowing which behavior is loving, and why it benefits us in every way can be confirmed in a very short time by our practice of loving principles. There is no other road to recovery and happiness. If the purpose of life is to enjoy it and share this enjoyment with others, there is no reason we should enjoy living or thinking in an unloving manner. Our living a loving life brings us joy; an unloving one does not. In a sense we spy on ourselves and our self-esteem is based on what we believe to be our true value not only to ourselves but also to others.

There is no fire and brimstone, scolding, or blind trust of traditional religious values in this book. But there is a firm connection with what some would call God's will for our lives. Here our definition of God is the power that creates and sustains reality and because our reality rules and principles work is therefore the source of our "higher-powered" principles. We present them as agnostic, but they are also consistent with the learning of most Biblical scholars.

Our solution is our learning to trust in constructive principles through our logic and experience, but not blindly swallowing someone else's faith. For those of us who have suffered greatly, this method seems to work best. Our experience in living by loving principles and our suffering are opposites. One heals us; the other disables us. We sufferers have to find our way back to wellness through experiencing a positive reality for ourselves which will help us feel secure. From that we can feel loving towards others and ourselves. It's the reverse process of how we lost our trust, suffered fears needlessly, and became ill. We experience this love by living and thinking by these loving principles and seeing what happens to us as a result.

Our Journey Through the Third Gate

In the 12-step fellowships they say they wish to "turn our will and our lives over to the care of God as we understood him." The words "as we understood him were added later as it became evident that so many of us had no firm belief in "God" as defined by religions. Here also, we wish to point out that a belief in a "God" is not necessary to recovery, but a belief that we can manage our lives in certain positive ways to achieve the best results is necessary. For this reason we offer the reality rules and positive principles as the guideposts for managing our lives. They are based on two ideas: we must not believe or invent ideas which contradict reality as we experience it or we will be unable to experience the faith we need to get us well. We affirm through positive principles that our world is navigated best by people who are willing to try to live by loving principles. We don't do this because any religion has told us to, even thought they all do; we accept this guide toward our thoughts and actions because experience shows these ideas work best in our real world.

Are These the Right Principles For You?

Take a look at your problems and try to see what would happen if you lived by the above principles and reality rules. Do you see a match-up of problems to solutions?

You might begin to see that all of our problems are addressed to some degree by them. After I began to use them to help people get well, I also discovered they were found directly or by implication in almost all of the holy scriptures. The Torah, The New Testament, the Koran, in Hindu and other Eastern teachings, as well as Native American and other spiritual teachings. Is this just coincidence? No. They have survived because they work. For thousands of years people have found that they are effective. I have, too.

You have to decide that for yourself. These are the ones that have worked for me and so many of my friends. Remember that the Third Gate has nothing to do with established religions, but rather with helping us guide our thoughts, feelings and behavior. If the idea of changing the way you live is uncomfortable or confusing, don't worry. We all found this a challenge or we'd have never gotten ill in the first place.

Just try it, and hope that it works for you, too. Millions of people have found that they work, and besides, what's the alternative? We could try to write our own moral code but, in a way, we're repeating the past if we do so. We have already decided once that we were wise enough to make up a path of wisdom as we went along. We often changed it to suit ourselves out of convenience or fears. Do you really believe that this time you can do it better? We hope that you won't need any more suffering to decide to join us and get well.

What About God?

Alcoholics Anonymous calls our Higher Power, God. We will often use this word to mean the Creator of the Universe. Let's not fall into the trap of meaning what people believe of God. We must always stick with what we can say we believe of God, or our resolve will fail when we need it most. Some who were taught to believe in a just and loving God became fearful and angered when they discovered, "Bad things happen to good people." We know we can not control the outcomes of our actions, but by living by positive principles and sound reality rules we also know we will be doing the best we can do to have a happy and secure life.

What we are ready to believe today may, and probably will be, different from what we come to believe in the future. The joy of feeling free and loving opens up in us a gratitude that gives us an acceptance of life as it is, even when it seems different from what we'd hoped.

Everyone's Holy Scriptures Tell Us Many of the Same Things

Most people know what they mean when they say "The Holy Bible," but to different people this has different meanings. Christians usually think of the "New Testament," and usually also mean, the "Old Testament," which for Jews is neither new nor old, but simply "The Torah." Jews also include in the Holy Bible, the Talmud, and for Jewish scholars, the Prophets, the Book of Esther, Judges, and even the commentary on each of these created by the leading Jewish scholars of all ages. Buddhists consider the writings of Buddha holy, and Hindu's have their Bhagavad-Gita and for some the Vedic scriptures. The Muslim bible is the Koran combined with the Torah (the Old Testament) and portions of the New Testament. There is a good reason why so many major religious groups accept the sacred scriptures of the others as holy. Concerning almost all matters or actions and attitudes in our daily lives they are all offering so much of the same wisdom.

In the creation of the Five Gates Program I used principles from the Torah, Talmud, and when this task was completed, I discovered that the Five Gates Principles and Reality Rules were also consistent with the Kabbalah as well as the sacred scriptures of all the other major religious groups, including those of Native Americans and the Toltec priestly class ("The Four Agreements"

© 1997 by Miguel Angel Ruiz, M.D.). At the time I created the Five Gates Program my familiarity was limited to the Torah, Talmud, and the New Testament; later I repeatedly discovered the joy of there consistencies and parallels with all the others.

Examples from the Torah (the Old Testament)

In Genesis we are told that Adam and Eve were forbidden from eating the "apple" of a certain tree, which scholars have told us is the tree of knowing "good" from "evil." They lived in an emotional and mental state of bliss until they violated this rule. In the Five Gates program we parallel this idea when we accept we have only one power and therefore only one job in life, "to try to do our best to know and do the next right thing"; that our problem is that we want to control everything and this forces us to believe we can control outcomes instead of humbly accepting that we can only try to do our best at managing ourselves well. We also deceive ourselves into believing that we can change the past or know the future, which was also not given to us as a power. Our poor self-esteem is caused by our preoccupation with judging ourselves instead of just managing ourselves the best we can. Still we need more direction than these ideas alone. We need self direction guide posts for managing our lives, for trying to figure out what is the next right thing to do, and what are the wisest methods for doing it.

But first, more on the issue of our natural resistance to limiting our expectations of ourselves to simply the best self-management of which we are capable.

In Genesis the Bible tells us that "Moses was the humblest of men." But when Moses prayed for divine help in overcoming the injustices he saw in Egypt, God came to him in the desert with specific directions on what he should do to overcome them, Moses showed that despite his being the humblest of men, he still questioned God and that he feared the outcome of his following those directions ("there are many powerful Gods in Egypt"); "How will I be able to persuade them that YOU are the one true God?" Moses wanted to know the future instead of what he asked for when he asked God's help. The Bible tells us in the English translation that he was answered; "*I AM THAT I AM!*"

This translation from the Hebrew text actually says *I SHALL BE AS I SHALL BE!* I interpreted this to mean that Moses was told to just follow God's directions if he had faith that he was being directed by the One true God. I believe that he was actually being told, "*Follow my directions and accept that the knowing of the future, the outcomes of my instructions, belong only to me.*"

Throughout Exodus we see many examples of Moses' being unwilling to simply follow God's directions with faith. Yet, earlier we were told that he was the humblest of men. This tells us something important about our nature. Humans have a hard time being humble and an even harder time achieving complete faith even when we are faced with the most absolute proof. This may be why the scripture goes on to tell us that the Hebrews are a "stiff-necked" people. This comment seem to apply to all of us.

We are further told that good will overcome evil by our being commanded to accept that creation was the result of God's positive intentions ("...and it was good") and that we are not to confuse negative actions and thoughts to be the proper way to achieve the most positive of intentions (Talmud). From this and many examples I have drawn from life, I have fashioned the principles and reality rules of the Five Gates to all be positive and to rely upon the simple truth that positive outcomes are best achieved by positive attitudes and actions.

Once again we find affirmations in the Holy Bible that our only jobs in life are to have faith that God's plan is positive, inevitable and all inclusive.

These are only a few of the major areas where the Five Gates' Principles and Reality Rules are consistent with the teachings of all peoples. Confirmation with this will have to lie with other scholars.

Faith is the Key

Your good intentions and your willingness to work hard to learn wisdom in order to bring about positive results in the world is the central commandment of all the bibles. We are told the importance of our having faith in a positive destiny governed by a positive creator. Even the ultimate dark side force personified by Lucifer or the devil is described to us in some scriptures (not the Torah explicitly) as the work and state of a fallen angel, whose ego fears caused him to rebel and question the supreme importance of God's wisdom, commanding us to employ love and positive actions in all the affairs of our world. We are told that love and constructive actions will prevail over fears, doubts and willful destructiveness.

But faith in what? In the Five Gates' philosophy we accept that when we are suffering from our seeing a negative world surrounding our inadequate self, we cannot accept faith in a loving creator. The reason we are suffering is that we do not have faith that everything is, was, and will be exactly as it is supposed to be, since we have no power to change the past or the future but only have a limited power to manage ourselves in the present. Our other judgments and unrealistic self expectations are what get us in emotional and mental trouble. As young children we were taught to believe that we must know or do even those things we cannot know and those things we cannot do.

Our spiritual condition is eroded by our resulting fears, and we experience anxieties and the hopelessness of depression. In the Five Gates' Philosophy we accept that when we experience this condition intensely and especially early in our lives, it is the cause of our obsessive compulsive disorders including addictions, which in many ways drive almost all of our mental and emotional disorders; attention deficit disorder ("Avoidance Syndrome," our name for ADD), bipolar disorder (addiction to false self-assuring ideas to try to combat our depressions), narcissism (an addiction to beliefs of personal disconnection with the well being of others), and many others.

What's More Important, Study or Practice?

Understanding these ideas intellectually helps, but without a lot of practice applying these principles, intellectual understanding is not enough to get us well. As we examine each idea, we think about situations in which it might apply, and then try them out. The results won't always be "good" in the sense that we'll get the result we wanted. This is true even if we could live this perfectly, or any other way of living, perfectly (can we ever know if we have managed ourselves perfectly?). The answer is that we must always gratefully accept reality. Even when the result isn't pleasing to us, we accept it as being right. This takes time, practice, honesty and an open mind.

Through practicing this way of life, we will eventually see that when we do all we can reasonably to act in accordance with constructive principles, this is in itself the only good result we need, no matter how any particular situation turns out. Our acceptance of this one idea is a critically important key in our program. Saying it is easy, but doing it takes lots of study, practice, vigilance, and courage. In time, it will become as habitual a way of thinking as our old less effective ways were. Then life gets relaxed and pleasurable.

Examples of the Third Gate In Action

The first time you come through the Third Gate, you are still in the orientation phase of your Five Gates Core Training. Your objectives at this stage of your development is considerably narrower than they will be when you come through the Third Gate again (this follows the Fifth Gate spiritual awakening). At this stage, we simply want to get the taste and feel of some of the positive principles and reality rules which you will be using later to keep yourself in good spiritual condition. Life will inevitably present you with challenges by tempting you to fall into your old patterns of thought and resulting behavior. As you practice using these rules and principles to manage all situations in your life, they will eventually become natural to your way of thinking. This is our goal.

Some examples are as follows:

- We went to a social gathering and tried to make friends, or a date, with someone who rejected us. This is not really a serious threat to our lives, but may negatively impact our spiritual condition unless we correctly identify the principles that will assure us that everything is just fine. We need to see that we have done a positive thing by reaching out, and the person who was unreceptive had his or her own reasons, perhaps their own undisclosed inabilities to link up with us in a positive way. We need to remember one of our most important reality rules: "What I believe, feel, think and, therefore, do are about me. What someone else believes, feels, thinks and does is actually about them, even if they say, or we are tempted to believe, it is actually about us" (We must independently make up our own minds about that). Other principles would apply here, but at this stage we simply want to see that we need tools to remind ourselves not to take the bait of self-judgment when we don't receive the affirmations we want, or even experience the rejections of others.

- We have just learned that our home has been burglarized, and our natural instinct is to feel terrible about ourselves, thus destroying our good spiritual condition or self-esteem. We must remind ourselves here that our only job in life is to manage ourselves in this present moment in time, and to decide to do the next right thing now and not try to hold on to how we could of, should of, would of changed the past. Changing the past is something we can no longer do now, anyway. We have numerous principles that apply to this example, but I am sure we can all agree that beating ourselves up over the fact that we didn't anticipate this event, or letting ourselves descend into the negative realm of anger, accusations or other negative emotions, will not help us as much as just getting on with what we must do to enjoy and operate effectively in this moment of time. That's all that can help us. This principle applies to all kinds of losses.

- We applied for a job we know we are very well qualified to do, but the person making the decision does not see it that way. Getting this job meant a lot to us, as it would have answered many of our perceived needs. We could take the ego bait and either feel sorry for ourselves or angry with the decision-maker who rejected our application. But these responses to this situation would steal from us our even more precious possession, our good spiritual condition. Instead, we must refocus ourselves in present time, and simply learn what we can from what is unchangeable, the past. We must learn, reassess and act positively, coming from a place of gratitude, giving thanks for what we already *do* have, and holding onto our hopes that our needs will be fulfilled in other ways at other times. The one need we are certain to have is the need to feel fine right now, so we cannot only enjoy this moment, but focus on making good decisions and taking positive actions toward our positive goals.

In all of these cases, we really have the same problem and the same principles. Our problem lies in our expectations and belief that things are not as they are supposed to be. Our natural tendency is to be disappointed which pulls us out of present time and makes us want to believe that we can change the past or do more than simply manage ourselves to our best ability in the present.

We can learn from a dog whose paw is caught in a trap. It will not think like a human being. It will not think about how it got stuck in this trap or any of the problems it will face if it can't get free. It will just think about getting free, even if it has to bite off its own paw. Human beings, on the other hand, will not only think of many distracting considerations, but many more, including why that idiot farmer left his wolf trap where his own dog would get caught in it! In order to keep our good spiritual condition, we must learn to think like the dog. Each time we face what we think is a serious problem, we can do constructive things that the dog can not do. We can decide how bad a problem is and what it will be worth to free ourselves from it. But whatever importance we decide to give our problem, we must stay positively focused in the present time, redirect our expectations away from what people outside ourselves will do or not do and *accept* that our only job in life is to manage ourselves in this moment with an eye toward a more positive future toward which we will contribute our positive feelings, intentions, creative planning and actions. We can solve our problems by doing some things the dog can't do. But we must also learn from the dog's sharp focus on solving its present problem.

Our natural instinct will be to reject these ideas as being maybe too idealistic. We may even decide we cannot achieve this level of objective focus in the present, even though these ideas may look right to us. We may even appear less human by rationalizing so objectively, mistakenly believing that we are supposed to submerge our pointless emotions. We may mistakenly become distracted by our natural tendency to mourn our losses instead of reminding ourselves of our blessings. Some will even tell us mourning is a necessary part of dealing with our losses. Once we have completed our Fifth Gate, we will know better. Even in our partial achievement of living by some of this enlightenment, we will improve our lives to the extent that we work towards enlightenment so that our growth will continue throughout our whole lifetime. Our greater clarity will not diminish our humanness, but instead will give us feelings of great well-being which will drive our love and generosity.

We will go into this more thoroughly in the following section, with emphasis on the specific Five Gates tools that we must then work towards mastering so we will not give up the wonderful spiritual awakening that will be ours at the conclusion of the Fifth Gate.

On the brighter side, as we gain our ability to control our negative emotions and support our excellent spiritual condition, all of the positive blessing of our lives will eventually outweigh the negative. We will have so many positive options stemming from our new positive spiritual condition that a casual rejection at play or work will mean less and less to us, and we will be more and more attractive to everyone, most importantly to ourselves, in every way without fear. We learn to lock our doors and buy insurance where it is warranted, and we will keep our paws out of many kinds of traps by consciously watching where we tread. But when life throws us a challenge, our positive spiritual condition, combined with our positive spiritual principles will keep us happy, powerful, and supremely capable of managing our lives.

I have always admired the New Orleans custom of throwing a joyous party for funerals, the Shaolin Monks' rejection of holding onto worldly things, and most of all, the person whose expectations gives them the fewest circumstantial needs. I especially admire the person who reaches into him-or herself to find love for everything and everyone without the slightest concern about who loves them back. We will be much more ready to understand and accept this level of spiritual enlightenment after we have completed our Fifth Gate. For now, before you have taken your Fifth Gate, this guidance and the promise that you will need to be able to master even more powerful tools for managing your life is all you need for now to understand the Third Gate.

How Can I Know If I Have Successfully Journeyed Through the Third Gate?

The secret to the Third Gate lies first in our intentions. We stated with the conviction that came from our understanding of the First and Second Gates that we do not want to manage our lives by fearful ideas any longer. Instead, we wish to guide our thoughts and actions by positive principles and reality rules.

After we complete the Core Training, which consists of our first time through each of the Five Gates followed by our more enlightened review of the first Three Gates, we begin to put our new enlightenment to work managing our lives. We strive to learn more and more so that we can do this more effectively, and we renew our Third Gate commitment on a continuous basis. If we ever lose this commitment, we will begin to slide backward into the world of fears instead of moving forward into the light of greater satisfaction and happiness. For now, all we need to complete our Third Gate successfully is to know in our hearts that we accept our desire to try our best to live by positive principles.

<u>THE FOURTH GATE</u>

I Must Learn About My Reality

Statement of the Fourth Gate:

"My present is the result of my past. To understand it and myself best, I must carefully review what I can remember of my history."

- *"My present..."* Although in our Fourth Gate we try to discover all the facts we can about our past, it is our self in the present we are trying to heal.

- *"...is the result of my past..."* Not only are our personalities at each stage of our development caused by the effects of our experiences and the beliefs we drew from them, but also even our hereditary legacy is part of our history.

- *"...To understand it and myself best..."* We do not strive for understanding our history as we are journeying through the Fourth Gate, even though we may see interesting and often valid connections. Instead, we simply focus on the job of recording our history so that we can have the ammunition we need to do the job of understanding ourselves as we journey through the Fifth Gate.

- *"...I must carefully review..."* If we were given the task of writing our history in any form that seems natural to us, we would probably write a very distorted version that omits some of the most important facts we are seeking here. Instead, we use a questionnaire which may be imperfect to fit our exact lives, but which gives us the best chance to catch the events, feelings, ideas, and actions in the order in which we remember experiencing them. By doing it this way, we have the greatest chance of not skipping the things we would otherwise choose to ignore, or which we don't know yet matter.

- *"...what I can remember..."* We try our best to remember all we can to answer to the questions of the Fourth Gate questionnaire. We note, but do not trouble ourselves, about the things we can't remember. Stop where it seems surprising that you can't remember a period of time or the circumstances of what you believe is an important event. You will use this information in the Fifth Gate to see if perhaps you have blocked those memories.

- *"...from my history."* As we journey through the Fourth Gate we record what we can remember of our thoughts, feelings, events (even our dreams), and actions one at a time in sequence as we lived them.

Why We Need to Learn the Truth of the Fourth Gate

Before we take our journey through the Fourth Gate, we could never tell anyone our life story with any objectivity. For the sake of preserving our egos, we always hold onto our "story" in a form that we want to believe it but not always consistent with the real facts. In the Fourth Gate we're not asked to tell our story, but instead we are asked to answer specific questions from which we will be able to begin constructing our real story when we take our Fifth Gate healing journey.

Purpose of the Fourth Gate

Wrongly, we started believing that we *are* our history; that we are nothing more than our habits and traits, and we start condemning ourselves. We decide there's something wrong with us, so deeply buried that we lose hope it can be changed, that the things we fear about ourselves can be seen in a new more accurate perspective.

The purpose of our journey through the Fourth Gate, followed by our journey through the Fifth Gate, is for us to clearly see how much power we really have and how little we need to judge ourselves or anyone else. How incredibly exhilarating it is for once in our lives to be focused on the present. This is the greatest high we'll ever have, and anytime we start to lose that high we can have it right back.

We pass through the Fourth Gate by examining our past. We may have feelings that come back up for us that were buried a long time ago and we don't really want to go back to. This is all normal, natural, expected and wonderfully productive. We simply need to follow the instructions, and we will create a detailed map of all the important transitional moments in our lives to the best of our ability at this time.

Truth of the Fourth Gate

The greater part of the truth of our Fourth Gate will be unknown to us until we have completed our Fifth Gate. In our performance of the Fourth Gate, we accept that we are the product of our lives and that if we wish to change the course of our lives, we must know our history. This is so that in the Fifth Gate, we can take the dramatic, transformational realignment of our life's directions in order to become our most happy and effective selves.

We accept that prior to taking our Fifth Gate we can't know for sure which parts of our history are most and least important, and so we try our very best to be as honest and thorough as we can be in gathering together the raw material and the facts of our lives. We accept that in our Fourth Gate, many of the facts, even important facts, are blocked from our conscious memories or perhaps were not lastingly recorded because we weren't aware of their importance at the time. These missing facts from our conscious memories are most likely to be revealed during the transformational process of the Fifth Gate.

Our Journey Through the Fourth Gate

In this gate, and the one to follow, we hope to accomplish certain things:

1. We will see ourselves as being the result of our lives. We accept that for better or worse, we grew up with attitudes and

feelings given to us by our environments. These feelings led to our values, trusts, fears, and our constructive and destructive behavior toward others and us. We did not get ill alone, and this helps us understand that we need new insights and healthier interactions with others. In the Fourth Gate, we see the great importance we play in each other's lives.

2. We will learn to forgive ourselves for our past deeds, and rededicate ourselves to a new, more positive way of living without useless fears, guilt or distraction.

3. In our understanding of why we can forgive ourselves our past and recent conditions, we learn that we can forgive all others, too: past, present and future. We realize that we cannot hate other people, but we may hate some of the things they do.

4. We will see clearly how to be part of the solution to our problems, and to the world's problems, instead of being one of their causes.

5. We will see for ourselves exactly how we function emotionally and mentally, and realize that we can get well if we can find the courage to work our program as best we can. We no longer have to take anyone else's word for it. The Fourth Gate brings our hope to its highest level of fulfillment.

6. We will learn to smile inside, perhaps for the first time in quite a while, as a great weight is lifted from our hearts.

How to Work the Fourth Gate

Once you start working this Gate, don't stop until it's done unless absolutely necessary. Our risk of relapse is greatest here, with only part of the Gate done. If we stop in the middle, we get the problems without the solutions. In short, our shame and unrelieved pain may just drive us to an even lower self-image. This brings us more suffering, and may cause us to revert to the use of our addictions for relief. Our recovery is a matter of life and death for most of us, so setting aside a couple of whole, undisturbed days to work Gate Four is highly recommended.

We use the outline provided on the following pages because it helps us to be certain that we did not avoid any issues important to a thorough accounting of our lives and feelings. Please read through all the directions of Gate Four before starting. We recommend that they be read more than once, until they are perfectly clear.

The first goal of the Fourth Gate is to find the events or ideas that impressed us positively or negatively, and made us fearful or safe as small children, starting from as early an age as possible. We do the same for our adolescence and early adulthood, and if we are older than 35, our later adulthood. We are especially careful to note all of our feelings, perceptions, and details, as they seemed at that time. The periods just before, during and after our periods of addiction, or periods of severe depression, anxiety or other suffering, are all-important. Also, we should not leave out our happiness and joy, including those good feelings we got from the use of our obsession or addiction of choice. We should make a particular note as to when they occurred and when they didn't. Try to see what we wanted from them and what changed over time. When we have checked our work for honesty, completeness and accuracy, we are done with the Fourth Gate.

We recommend that you use a word processor if your writing is problematic, although you are the only person who will ever need to read your Fourth Gate answers. Most important is that you get into an isolated environment for as long as it takes to finish. Usually, a few sessions of an hour or more are sufficient for most people. Don't try to come to causal conclusions as you write, since you may invent wrong reasons for why things happened, and this can diminish the effectiveness of this Gate. Be razor honest and as thorough as you can be.

Once you're sure that you've finished, take the Fifth Gate as quickly as possible. It will take about half as long as the Fourth Gate. If you are going to use the help of another person for taking the Fifth Gate journey, pick someone you trust, someone who is wise about people, and who has recovered from past suffering themselves. You can take yourself through the Fifth Gate by following the instructions carefully.

What Is This Great Truth That Heals Us?

If you're able to follow these ideas this early in your recovery, you will probably ask, "How can a truth I don't like, or which has been scaring me, make me feel better by my seeing it clearly?" The answer is that our program teaches us that if this truth led us to destructive behavior or suffering, that it was a reaction from our fears and based on our misunderstandings about life, all of which we can correct. Our problem is always our inability to accept as fine our natural limitations and the true purpose of our lives, which is to enjoy life, grow wiser, and add to the enjoyment of life for others. When we don't see this simple truth, it sets us up for all of our problems with life and others.

In the Five Gates Training Program, we learn that we don't need to worry about what we can't help. Instead, we can feel great by doing something about the things we can help. We also learn that we never need to be or feel helpless if we are willing to see and reject certain wrong ideas. Our happiness does not take away anyone else's. It adds to it, if we have the right focus on how to see things.

We're also not responsible for what we can't help, such as our eventual human mortality or other limitations. When we're doing the best we can, we're completely adequate, and need not worry. By applying these simple, but powerful truths, we can clean up the results of our insanities and help ourselves to enjoy life.

Fourth Gate Inventory General Directions

Get paper and pen, or open a blank page on your word processor, and start writing. Writing things down helps connect us more with our feelings and memories, and causes us to focus more intensely and honestly. What we write we also read, knowing that it is private communication from us to ourselves.

The longer we wait to take our Fourth and Fifth Gates, the longer we suffer needlessly and the greater the risk that we will relapse. The more thoroughly we search for the answers to these questions, the greater the relief we will receive. Make no compromises with this step that you don't want to make with your whole effort to find joyful recovery.

Do not suspect that anyone, not even you, will use any of this information against you in any way. The purpose is to finally share it honestly and fully, to be healed of its pain, and then to get on with our new, constructive lives, finally free of our fear, guilt, shame, anger, resentments, cravings and remorse.

The Fourth Gate inventory is for your eyes only. If you're going to use the services of a facilitator you are going to tell them about it, but writing it down and reading it is just for you. There is no extra credit for good handwriting, spelling or style, just for truth and completeness. Don't erase or cross out anything. Often, these "slips" are clues to otherwise hidden truths. Don't worry that you've got some awful secrets that must stay hidden. We find that we are as "sick as our secrets." Besides, few of us have any really great ones anyway. Our guilt and shame only make us think we do.

Write out the resentments, fears, feelings of guilt, hates, sex hang-ups or unusual lusts and fantasies you can remember. What you want to be aware of most is your reaction to what happened to you. An inventory deals with feelings more than events, both good and bad. An example is: "I resented my mother because she loved my brother more," or "I hated my father for punishing me in front of my friends," or "I used to tell on my brother so I'd look good to my parents." Get it all, and any connections you believe were true. What we used to feel and believe can give us key insights.

If you find that any question awakens some painful or distressing memory, write it down, even if it's not an answer to a particular question. If you feel any statement you wrote is wrong, make a note as to why you feel it is wrong.

Some people have been discouraged in taking an inventory because they don't feel they have become honest enough, or can remember everything that happened to them. Write down periods of time or events you remember poorly, because they may provide clues to buried feelings. Don't worry! No one is capable of remembering every event of his or her life. Write down what you are capable of remembering now. More will come out later, especially as you go through the Fifth Gate. Keep in mind that in the Fourth Gate we change nothing. We just tell ourselves our secrets. An inventory is only a story of our beliefs, feelings and actions from our birth until now, not a judgment.

Most of our mental and emotional patterns start in our childhood and early adolescence. Your inventory therefore will be divided into three or four parts: Childhood, Adolescence, Early Adulthood and, if you're over 35, Later Adulthood. Our parents and close family members are the most likely suspects in our search for finding out what happened to us and how it changed us. Later, we usually kept the ball rolling, transferring or acting out our maladjustments or peculiar beliefs or fears to many of our later relationships and situations.

One of the most common problems we remember is our parents making us feel guilty or inadequate by one statement, attitude or another. Look for these situations; they are keys! Another of our common problems comes from our parents teaching us not to express our feelings or to cry. Usually this stems from their inability to handle our feelings, often even their own.

Let this unfold naturally. If you're not sure of an answer, just say so. Don't worry. You're about to become free of all this garbage. Keep in mind that these questions were designed to try to make sure they covered almost everyone. Don't become discouraged if some do not apply to you.

Be Your Own Five Gates Trainer

In this version of the Fourth Gate Questionnaire, we have incorporated special notes at the end of certain questions. First answer the question without looking to the notes. Then read the note on that question if there is one. The purpose of this is to give you a head start in helping you take yourself through the Fifth Gate. If you like, you can add to your answers additional information that the notes suggest to you. Also, be sure to make a note on your answer to remind yourself if you had any special feelings as you answered each question. These notes about your feelings will help you identify the areas in which you may have unresolved issues that you will want to pay special attention to as you take yourself through the Fifth Gate. This version of the Fourth Gate requires much more work on your part because you are asked to be you are your own Trainer. Our intention is to make it possible for you to experience the healing freedom and empowerment of the Fifth Gate. When you take the Fourth Gate journey, as it is described here, you will feel the changes taking place within you as you discover the connections between who you are and how your life has shaped you. This will give you the power to change yourself into the happy and more powerful person you want to be. You are asked to do this difficult job once but you will receive the benefit of it throughout your life. It's well worth it.

Childhood

1. Write down your notes about what you know about your mother's (or female guardians') parents' lives, including their personalities and beliefs. If you had more than one maternal guardian in your childhood, you should answer this question for each one as though each of them had in some sense been your mother. You want to write down everything you know about the home your mother grew up in, changes going on at the time she was a child, what she believed or possibly argued against, the image she saw of how married people (her parents) lived together and related to each other and their children, and other family members, the community and the world in general.

2. How did your mother feel about herself? Her womanhood? Her motherhood?

Note: Try to see how, in as many ways as possible, you both think and feel a lot like your mother or grandparents, or how you struggled to reject those ideas and feelings.Remember, nothing's an accident! Everything about you that is true today, was caused by something in your past.

3. Answer the same questions about your father's parents and the home he grew up in, using the first question as a guideline.

4. Do you believe you were wanted at birth? Write out the circumstances of your family at the time of your birth, things such as family size, age differences and financial circumstances. Was there laughter? Arguing? Depression? Were other relatives or people living with you? How old were your parents? Was there anything else worth noting about your home just before or just after you were born?

5. Describe what you think your family thought of you as you grew up. Your brothers? Your sisters? Answer this question for each one.

Note: Be sure to take into allowance where your parents circum-stances may have changed during the period of time during the births of each of your brothers and sisters. Sometimes parents have treated their children differently because their lives were different at the time each child was raised. For example: Sometimes a younger child will be raised at a time in which the same parents had more money or may have learned something about raising their older children; sometimes their relationship with each other may have changed making a divorced father or mother less willing or able to give as much personal time or money, or more time and money to a later born child.

6. How old were you at the birth of brothers and sisters? How old were they when you were born? How did you feel about the new arrivals? Did anything in your parents lives change so that they may have felt differently about having another child?

7. Was either of your parents sick enough to need hospitalization? Otherwise sick? Anxious? Depressed? Insecure? Alcoholic or otherwise addicted? Compulsive? Obsessed with anything? Did either of your parents change in their mental or emotional health during the times between which you or any of your brothers or sisters were born? Raised?

8. Were you separated from any important family members? When? How? Did you feel fear or guilt about this separation? Did you feel responsible, angry, abandoned?

9. Were you threatened by the bogeyman? The devil? People of other races? No Santa Claus for you? With damnation if you misbehaved? If so, what were your fears in these matters?

10. Many of us have anxious attitudes about sex. Were you made to feel guilty about their normal sexual curiosity? Were you caught or punished for touching yourself or others or caught masturbating or playing "doctor?"

Note: Some parents tell children that sexual feelings are evil or bad and must be punished or avoided. Were you told your growth would be stunted, your hair would fall out, or other terrible things would happen?

Note: With no sex education, and given this sort of teaching, a child will naturally be confused or scared about sex. When a child is exposed to fully developed nude persons in the bathroom, at home or in public, or have seen others being sexual, they may begin to feel inadequate because they have not as yet developed, or guilty to see them. These feelings may carry over into feelings of inadequacy or shame in adult life, even when we are a fully-developed adult.

11. Write down any similar feelings or experiences related to these ideas that did or do make you feel uneasy. Describe it as much as you remember. You want to remember your feelings and not just what happened.

12. Were you told if you were good, only good things would happen to you? Were you good but did you still have bad things or disappointing things happen?

Note: Even if we tried to be good, life may have still delivered us grave disappointments. Some examples of this are, "If you go to Church every Sunday, you will have a good life," "If you complete school with good grades, you will have a good career and a good life," "If you marry a particular kind of person, you will have a good life," or other similar promises. We may have done these things and still grown up to be unhappy. Some people harbor great resentments for this reason. Do you have any? This question is very important because we usually do not become emotionally troubled by results we expected. What causes us to feel that life is unjust or that we are "losers" is when we think we have done the right thing and gotten an expected result from which we suffer. Take all the time you need on this question to see this aspect of yourself. Ask yourself, "Do I believe in my heart that the life I have was the result I expected from the things I did?" For most of us who need a program of healing and growth, the answer will be "NO!" As long as we believe that life is unjust, we can not get well or be happy. We must go back in our memory to discover why it is that we expected things to turn out differently. We must see that this happened to us because either life works differently than we were taught to believe it did, or we did things we haven't yet accepted as having caused our disappointing results, or we just haven't waited long enough to have our right actions to give us what we want. There is no fourth answer to our disappointments if we want to be happy. In our Fifth Gate you will be asked to see your disappointments and unproductive fears in the light of this truth. If you can't do it now, don't worry. It means that you will have to do this job in the Fifth Gate. Remember that not all people work the same way. Sometimes you can even be good to someone and they are unable to give you the result you want because of something about them and not you.

13. Did you have a love for doing something you may have wanted to pursue, possibly make your career? Sometimes people are told they should stop being serious about their art, music, passion for athletics, or writing. Do you have bad feelings about having given up activities which you now greatly regret, possibly now even resent? Write this down including who it was who told you had to give them up?

14. Were you taught to believe that your thoughts and feelings did not count? Even if this wasn't said to you directly, the way your parents behaved may have given you this message. If so write down this part of your childhood experience. If your answer to this question is yes, ask yourself "what do I know about the person who made me feel this way?" This

attitude was about them and not about you. Try to see why that person might have felt this way.

15. Some of us were touched sexually when we were small, or made to touch others. If at the time we had believed that this was wrong, or didn't know and enjoyed it, or felt uncomfortable, this may have had a strong effect on us. We children may have enjoyed it, but were told later that it was a terrible thing that happened to us. As the result we may have hurt by losing trust in an adults or specifically men or women. If anything like this happened to you in childhood, please describe it in detail. What happened? Who was involved? How did it make you feel at the time it was happening? What were you told to believe about it? How did you feel about it?

Note: This question is not only about sexual things, but could be about violence or dishonesty. Think about how anything you were taught or made to do wrong as a child may have caused bad behavior or bad feelings in you today. You need to know that not all the things you are inclined to do have come from your own desire to do anything wrong. This could even include drinking or drugs or any negative habits or values you may have. Think about where in your youth these patterns or values may have been started.

16. Were you afraid of the dark? What happened? Did you lose sleep? Become nervous? If your fear was caused because you couldn't see what was going on, this is a natural concern, but if your fear of the dark was taught to you because someone taught you to fear the dark, then it is worth noting. Sometimes fearful people will teach us to be afraid of things when we're small even though today we can see there is no logical fear to be afraid of them.

Note: This question is not only about fearing the dark. Maybe you fear getting into elevators or walking into closed places like a closet or a room without windows or being unpopular or poor financially or having parents that don't have money. Stop to consider all of the atti-

tudes that you have grown up with that don't make sense to you logically now but still apart of how you feel today. We all have many of these and some of them can be at the root of our dysfunctional attitudes, feelings, and behavior. Psychologists call some of them phobias because we fear things for which there is no logical cause, but if we understood the messages of our childhoods well enough, we would see the cause. Most of us can't do that, but it's enough to know that nothing about us is an accident and that none of the things that are a part of us from our early lives could possibly be our fault.

17. Were you afraid to fight? Or not to fight because of pressure from your family? Did your inclination to fight or not to fight have a negative effect on your life. Who taught you about fighting? What did they say or do? How did this affect your relationships with other kids?

Note: All of us have had at times in our lives the tendency to be too combative or too passive. All this means is that we thought at that time that this was the best way to solve our problems or be who we were supposed to be. Think about how you may have been too aggressive or too passive in situations in your life, and if possible, who's words or example may have taught you to be this way. This question is not only good for childhood, but it is an important aspect of our personality and behavior that we may need to understand about each phase of our lives. Try to see how this aspect of yourself influenced your life and where those ideas came from.

18. How did your parents punish you? Did they try to reason with you, or limit your privileges or freedom? Was it physical? Was it severe? Did you feel it was unnecessary or unfair? Did they punish you to control you? How did it work? Do you have co-dependency problems today? Are you to harsh a disciplinarian with other people? Employees? Friends? Your children?

Note: Co-dependency is the description of how some people are overly concerned about how other people react to them. Sometimes, this condition can be so severe that people do self-destructive things (or fail to help themselves by not doing important things) because they fear not being accepted or loved by others. If you have a co-dependence problem or you have noticed this problem in others around you, unnecessary punishment may be the cause. Keep in mind that we all do the things we do because we think they are right and not because we want to harm them. Stop to consider how much the way you were disciplined as a child may have influenced the way you deal with subordinates, friends, loved ones, or children today. Most important, stop to consider if you have created this problem in others, whether or not you meant them harm or were just doing what you were taught was right. Stop to consider whether or not you believe those who had authority over you were really trying to harm you or just doing what they thought was right. One form of punishment is refusing to love or accept another person for who they really are. Don't we all do this to some extent? If we want to be free and happy, we must allow others to be free and happy too and not decide that we know what's best for them. In raising our children, we are all faced with trying to balance shaping them in responsible ways but also allowing them to feel loved, accepted, and free to discover who they need to be for themselves.

19. What kind of marriage do you think your parents had? Affectionate, violent, argumentative, manipulative or complaining? Be sure to answer this question as completely as you can.

Note: This is a very important question because we all learn about love and how to express it and live happily with others from the successful and unsuccessful examples we saw as children, starting with our parents. It is not an accident that most abusive people are the children of abusive parents or that most happily married people are the children of happily married people even though there are many exceptions. Did your father or mother tell you that men or women were a certain way. If so, we probably believed them and not that that was just their experience. Homosexuals have a special need to look at this question and their answers with greater thoroughness since we all learn about love beginning with what we believed was successful or

unsuccessful in the probably heterosexual relationship between the two
key figures that shaped the world in which we were raised. Our
answers to these questions will help us to see and understand how we
grew up to be who we are in relation to the opposite or same sex. This
is not the only issue that homosexuals may wish to examine in this
regard, but it is for all of us an important part of how we relate in
intimate relationships. We all need to consider examining this aspect of
ourselves in understanding our patterns of loving. Are you living the
same pattern in one relationship after another? Why?

20. If they fought, did you resent it? Did it scare you? Were you
    used to break up or start their fights? To take one side or
    another? Were they so close to each other that you couldn't
    feel a part of them? Were they so close to each other you felt
    shut out?

Note: Again it is important to answer this question very thoroughly
because our relationships are the platform from which we go forward
to live our lives.

21. If your parents were from different religions, races, cultures,
    or economic backgrounds, did you feel confused or
    conflicted about it? Does this explain apart of how you feel
    today?

22. Were you afraid of storms? Other dangers? Does this explain
    anything about you today?

23. Can you remember feeling extremely lonesome at certain
    times in your childhood? Record all of these feelings and
    when they happen. Make a note of who was or wasn't a part
    of your everyday experience at that time. How did each
    important person contribute to your feelings of connections
    with others.

Note: Some of us have a hard time because we always seem to feel
alone or feeling that we can't be alone. This is always caused by how
we learned to relate to others when we were children. Consider this

aspect of yourself if isolation or narcissism may be a part of your make-up today.

24. Did anyone or maybe several people in your life tell you that you were bad? This question could apply to two different situations. "I was told that I was bad because I did...," or "I was told I was bad without specific reasons being given. Some of us were told we were bad because we were not good looking, too fat, weren't smart enough, sick too often, disabled, or even possibly we were too tall or too short. There is a major difference between being told you were bad because of things you could have changed and being told you were bad for things you couldn't. You could have been told you were bad for things that weren't even true because someone needed to believe this or to tell you this. Sometimes we can be told that there was something wrong with us because of who our father or mother was. Think back through your childhood memories to try to remember all the times and ways in which you were repeatedly told you were bad. In each case try to remember who told you this and then see if you can understand a reason why they may have said this that really was not about you, but more about them. Also, try to remember if you felt you couldn't help yourself, even though what they were saying was true of you. When we were told we were bad as children, our co-dependence naturally caused us to believe this and this can be a major source of how we could have grown up to feel inadequate.

Note: As you answer this question, keep in mind that all children, including us, are really trying to do their best even if it appears otherwise. Their is always a logical cause for everything we do and don't do. If you were bad as a rebellious adolescent, also keep in mind that some degree of this is natural to the process of our growing up to believe we have some degree of control and authority over ourselves even though we still may be dependent upon our parents or other authority figures.

25. List all the feelings of guilt, fear and resentment you had toward each person in your life as a child, which may not reflect your current feelings.

Note: Before you can become well you will need to reconcile your problem feelings toward everyone in your life. You may be able to do this as you take your Fourth and Fifth Gate. In some cases this reconciliation will automatically adjust later as your understanding of yourself and life deepens.

26. List the first time you ever stole anything. List all your thefts. Tell why you did it, if you know.

27. How old were you when you first masturbated? Were you ever caught and made to feel guilty? Did you feel guilty even though you weren't caught? Did you fear being caught?

28. What other sexual curiosity were you involved in (e.g., homosexual, animal, members of family, sodomy, or anything else)?

Note: The factual answers to this question and the proceeding one are of no importance. What's important is what you believed and possibly still believe deep down about these ideas or events. Very few physical acts or even impulses will have any lasting effect upon us. But we carry our beliefs around with us the rest of our lives unless we need to and successfully change them. Just keep in mind that we mustn't try to "fix what ain't broken." Sexual curiosity is a natural part of who we are.

29. If you were named after someone, what was that person like? Did you care? Why? Do you think it has had any effect on your life? If you think it was important, examine this aspect of yourself.

30. Did your family move often? If so, did you make friends and then have to break off the relationship so often that you became afraid to get too close? Did you resent having no say?

Note: Many children, especially adolescents, resent having no power over certain important decisions that affect them. If you have resentments about this, you may want to stop and consider what freedom your parents would have had to give up in order to give you the freedom you may have thought you deserved. This question could apply to other areas such as members of other races or religions who you would have liked to have as friends who could not enter your home, or you were told you did not have the freedom to keep as friends. Your parents may have felt that if you kept certain friends it would reflect unfavorably upon them and not only be bad for you. We don't need to decide what was right, we only need to see what was true and how it affected us. Did what you were taught then affect your life now? How? Do you want to change this?

31. Do you remember starting school? Keep in mind that when we were in school this may have been our whole world away from home. It's the place where we learned how we could make choices about managing our time, our friends, and who we wanted other people to believe we were. This is an important part of shaping the patterns of who we grew up to be. What were your feelings? Try to remember each successive grade in school and as you do write out the resentments and fears you felt toward teachers, kids, anyone. Fights, slights, embarrassments? Put them down. Did you feel like you didn't fit in? Why?

32. Did you resent your church, relatives, family friends or parents? If so, list them and your feelings. No resentment or fear is too small to mention. Resentments and fears are our greatest problems.

33. How did your parents talk? Were you ashamed of them? Dress? Education? Money? Grooming? Work? Car? Clothes? Home? Looks? Religion? Nationality?

Note: As you answer this question, stop to consider whether or not the answer may have disturbed you because you believed who they were was a definition of who you were. Have you yet learned that you are your own person able to talk, worship, dress, and choose friends, and all the rest the way you see fit? Do you see that you have a choice over who you are that can be independent of anyone else's including your parents. If this is one of your issues, accepting this truth is one of your most important goals in the Five Gates Training Program. This truth is one dimension of the truths of our First and Second Gates.

34. Did you ever see your parents in the nude? What were your feelings? How did they act? Angry? Okay?

35. Did you ever see or hear your parents having sex? What were your thoughts? Feelings?

Note: It's really not important whether you happened to see or heard your parents in a sexual situation even if was someone other than each other. What is important is whether or not this experience made you believe anything negative about yourself or life. Always ask yourself when looking at the answer to a question like this "Did I do anything wrong?" The answer is surely "NO." If there is a problem with this, the solution is in your seeing that what you saw or heard, even if you went out of your way to do it out of childhood curiosity, is not about you, nor is how anyone else felt about it.

36. In every family, a child usually has certain chores assigned. What were your chores? Did you think they were they fair or necessary? Could you do them? Could you please your parents?

Note: Our parents are fallible people just like us. They don't always know what we can or cannot do or how we feel about it, but sometimes our feelings of being unable of winning their appreciation or acceptance can become a disturbing influence in our early life self-esteem and even carried forward into our adulthood. Keep in mind that even in doing our homework, succeeding in school, or even controlling our bowels can be seen as part of our duties as children. If we wanted to do them or felt unable to do them, this was not our fault even though we were all told that it was because our parents were frustrated and didn't want to blame themselves for our failure to perform as they thought we should. Think about the early messages you got in life because you could or couldn't do what your parents thought you should. Maybe you didn't want to and neither they nor you knew why. There is a reason behind everything and the more reasons you can find the more surely and thoroughly you will heal yourself in this process. Sometimes, the reasons are just too far behind us for us to be able to find them. Then we need faith in the logical truth that we never meant wrong even when we couldn't do what others thought was right.

37. Did your parents seem to like your friends better than they did you? Did your friends seem to like your parents better than they did you? Did you resent this?

38. Were there any bad experiences at Sunday school? At summer camp? Relatives' homes? Friend's homes? Playing sports?

39. Were you an only child? Did you resent this or did you enjoy it? Were you overprotected so that you didn't get enough of a chance to learn about real life? How much of this was about you and how much of this was about your parents?

Note: As you answer this and other similar questions, keep in mind that you were never the author of who you grew up to be; you are the page on which the history was written and once you take yourself through the Fifth Gate you can come to a greater degree the author of your future.

40. Did your parents want a child of the opposite sex when they had you? Did they name or dress you like the other sex? Did they encourage in you the traits of the opposite sex by any of their attitudes?

Note: This question is about all of us to some degree, but it is especially important to homosexuals. We must see that this period in our lives was completely governed by our parents and not us including the attitudes and preferences we carried from it through our lives.

41. Did your appearance (looks, dress, etc.) embarrass you? Did you feel that you were "different" from your classmates? How?

42. Write any childhood memories that hurt you.

Use what you have learned to analyze the meaning of who did what and why and how that affected you. Sometimes things happen naturally without any human choice, like fires, floods, earthquakes or severe weather that may have gotten you or someone else physically harmed. Again, use what you've learned from the preceding questions to understand the influence this may have had upon you and why.

43. Which of the above questions about childhood was the toughest for you? Do you know why?

Adolescence

As small children, we were awed by and wanted to be accepted by our parents. As we approach adolescence, we begin to feel our separate identity growing within us. We seek more privacy and make a point of having our separate opinions, often becoming argumentative. Some of us feel a strange isolation as we make the separation from being our parents' little boy or girl to being a grown-up. We begin to see life as very competitive and this may scare us or make us cruel or ruthless. Sometimes, we are sneaky or dishonest. We crave new experiences, and believe we know what's best for us. This often makes us resent authority. To some degree, this is natural. While we are suffering we usually think of the causes as lying outside of ourselves and authority would not disturb us if we did not see it as the reason for our being unable to do what we believe is best for us.

We have to learn how to be self-managing and self-responsible. We're given responsibility by others, but often feel that our authority and resources are too limited. This troubles us and we may feel different and isolated. Our disloyalties make us feel guilty and ashamed while our frustrations can make us angry. This is all normal "stuff" and is just a part of growing up for many of us. But if these feelings are very extreme, they leave a mark on us, and often divert the direction of our lives.

Many adolescents and adults experience homosexual feelings, thoughts and acts. If there is guilt attached, more may be made of it than it deserves. Suffering from any fears regarding our sexuality can interfere with our self-esteem and ability to express ourselves sexually. A child who relies on the misguided sex information obtained from his playmates and friends can suffer a number of severe problems and desires, or lack of normal desires. Although these are often unconscious desires, they bring on conscious feelings of guilt. The more "normal" we are, the more we probably have had needless guilt feelings about common experiences. Let it all hang out. We've heard it all and then some. Maybe most of us have done it all, too. So what!

1. What has been your experience concerning the above? Distortions in our behavior and feelings are very common and important to know. Recognizing them will often help us get rid of the ones we don't want, and restore the ones we do want. For example, some girls are taught that men are interested in sex only, and some boys that the size of their penis is really important. These fictional ideas are destructive and damaging to a person. Have you experienced either of these attitudes? Is there a pattern? How has it affected you?

2. Did you have friends? What kind of friend were you? Did you really care about the others? Did you feel guilty about this? Did you care too much? Were you overly concerned about what others thought? When did this trait start? With whom?

3. What interest, or lack of interest, did you have in school? How was your social life? Did you participate in sports? What were the reasons for your participation, or lack of it? Were you good? At what? What were you not so good at?

4. Were you a troublemaker? If so in what way? Did you destroy property? Vandalism? Graffiti? Overly seek attention? What?

5. Did you resent leaders, either physical or mental? Did you resent not being the most handsome or beautiful person at

school? The smartest? Best groomed? Did you stutter? Wet your pants?

6. Did you feel you were a coward because you didn't want to fight? Did you like to fight? Were you a bully? Did you feel embarrassed because others made fun of you? Avoided you? Who did this? Why? Who didn't?

7. Were you exposed to other children in gym class or in the rest rooms who were older than you and more physically developed? How did you feel? Ashamed? Attracted? Inadequate? Scared? Some people feel inadequate as adults because they were exposed to youngsters more developed than they were at the time. If you feel uptight in this area, write about your feelings.

8. Did you resent not being part of a crowd? Or not being a leader? Or not being popular? Were you shy or outgoing? How are you now? Does any particular type of person make you shy? Afraid? Angry?

9. If you dropped out of school, explain your feelings and reasons. Did anything happen to you in high school that was a continuing source of shame? Fear? Anger?

10. Did your parents compare you to their family members, their friends or your friends? Did you resent them for wanting you to be like someone else?

Note: We all wanted the respect and love of our parents, and for this reason their opinions had great influence on us. If they gave us the message that we were supposed to be like someone else they were also telling us we were no good as we were. This can easily explain how we may have grown up with low self-esteem. We need to see these kind of causes clearly in order for us to understand how we may feel about ourselves today.

11. How did you get the attention of your family? Did you pout, sulk, be a good child, have temper tantrums, act like a dummy? Play sick? Get aggressive? Do you remember what kind of lies you told, if any? Figure out why, if you can.

12. How did you feel when you got caught lying? What was the most embarrassing incident of adolescence? Were there any others you really remember?

13. Did you used to run away from home? Why? Where did you run? Why there? Did you come back on your own? How did your family behave?

Note: If you ran away from home, your parents had two choices for how to behave when you returned: They could have tried to find out what was bothering you and make it clear to you that their home was your home no matter what and make you feel you were wanted there; instead, they could have put their emphasis on how it was wrong for you to run away. If they told you only that you were wrong, then they did you no good at all, even though their intentions may have been good for your well-being. Keep in mind the fact that your running away sent a message to them that they were inadequate as parents. This could explain why they may have behaved so insensitively toward you. Always remember, parents are just kids with more years of experience.

14. Were you jealous of others? Who? Why?

Note: Jealousy is a sure tip off that we feel bad about something about us. What was it? Do you still feel that way today? Why?

15. If sexy feelings were dismissed or put down in your family, there is a strong possibility that you will feel guilty about them today. We "catch attitudes." A boy who is pushed to always do better, or is criticized no matter what he does, may find himself having trouble in his sexual performance, or in other ways. A girl who has been told that it is not okay to feel sexy may grow up to dislike her own body and distrust her feelings, or react promiscuously to "show them," or get even. These attitudes create unnatural or uncomfortable sexual behavior. Did you "catch" any of these attitudes? Can you see it cropping up in your life now? Can you see the connections

between your family's attitudes and your attitudes and behavior?

16. First sexual intercourse: What were your feelings? Were you scared before you did it or afterwards? Why? Were you worried about not being adequate sexually? Most people are. Did you feel guilty? Did you feel disappointed? Be as specific about the feelings as you can. List in detail any homosexual experiences, masturbation fantasies, or other sexual activity you particularly remember. Keep in mind that we are not concerned about with whom, or on what date, or how often, but rather how did you feel about the experience. If you got someone pregnant, or became pregnant yourself, what did you do and how did you feel about your actions? Homosexuality? Pregnancy? Try to figure out the reasons for each of your feelings and whether or not you still have related feelings today.

17. Were you ashamed of your parents? Were they too old, too fat, too sloppy, too drunk, too whatever? Did you have the kind of clothes that other kids wore? Was there enough money for the things you needed? And if not, were you resentful of that? If there was, did you take it for granted? Did you feel any brothers or sisters got more than you did? Write out your feelings about money as an adolescent. Were you the kind of child you would want to have? Were you a thief? Were you ever double promoted? Left back? If so, did you have trouble adjusting emotionally? How did you act? How did you feel? Did you feel uncomfortable because you were superior or inferior to other students? Were you undependable as friend? Breaking off relationships without any explanation when something or someone who seemed better came along? Dislike yourself?

Note: This question is long and has many parts but each of them are related. Answer each part separately and if there is a problem aspect in your answer, try to figure out what was the source of your feelings. Keep in mind that our feelings are not about the facts of any situation especially if it was not under our control. Our feelings are governed by the differences between what we expect and what has actually happened. Look for the answer to what you expected and what you think happened and how it may affect your personality today. Many of these questions are repetitive for good reasons. We need to get into the habit of repeating the process of reminding ourself how we got to be who we are and how to see the real causes of our feelings and not just the events that took place around us. Once we get into this habit, not only the Fifth Gate but our daily maintenance into the Life Practice will become easier and easier. This is the source of our strength as graduates of the Five Gates Program. We learn to think accurately about the causes and the effects about all the issues in our lives both in the past and how they can teach us in how to deal with the present.

18. Did you pit one member of the family against another? Was it done to you? One friend or employee against another? One boyfriend or girlfriend against each other? How did you do this? Do you still do this today?

   Note: In this question you must be kind to yourself since experience shows that we learn all of these negative tactics from others. When we believe someone else is getting what they want or what we want by using these methods, we will naturally want to use them too. In the Five Gates Training Program we learn to believe in more positive methods in getting what we want and learn what we really need to be happy which is not always getting what everyone else wants. Real power comes from our learning how to be good to ourselves and other people and not manipulating them. When we employ this more positive point of view, we are relieved of the destructive struggle most of us have with the world around us, and our positive actions usually motivate others to be good to us.

19. What were your best experiences? The worst?
20. Is there anything that made you very uncomfortable when writing about it? Have you put down everything that has bugged you? Even the smallest things can be important. If they trouble you, put it down.

21. When you began your adolescence (11-13 years old), what did you think you were supposed to be like when you grew up? Personality? Lifestyle? With members of the opposite sex? Same sex? Do for a living? Professional? Educational achievements? How did these ideas about yourself change by the time you were eighteen years old? How did they change later? Did you feel like you needed to do things you couldn't do? Do you know what they are?

Note: As we have noted many times up to now, there are really three issues always operating in our lives: What we expect, what we think is happening, and what a more enlightened point of view can tell us about what is actually going on. The first two of these is usually all we cover in the Fourth Gate when we do it live with a certified Five Gates Trainer. In this self-administered Fourth Gate we have also included reflective exercises to help you begin to see the difference between our expectations, our perceptions at the time things are going on, and what insights you can gain into what was really going on. The truth is our path to freedom. By discovering much of the truth of these connections in the Fourth Gate, you have a big head start on the Fifth Gate. If there were parts you couldn't figure out, don't worry about it. They will come to you in the Fifth Gate anyway as we look at all of this information from a fresh, new perspective.

When Did Your Problems with Abuse or Addiction Begin?

We have abused substances like alcohol or other drugs, behavior like gambling, compulsive sexuality, lawlessness or violence, or any of many otherwise normal activities like eating. The possible list is endless, but each of us who have had a compulsive abuse or addiction problem knows about it. If you have had such problems, it will be very helpful to you if you can see how they influenced other aspects of your life such as your choice of friends, your economic circumstances, your health, feelings about yourself, or even your legal status. Usually, these problems are slow developing, but not necessarily.

When did you start using or abusing substances or other behaviors? What were the circumstances? What were your feelings at that time, especially just before and after you were using? What was the reason for the "use" To escape? Escape from what? Fit in? Feel more confident? Relax? Cope? Be brazen? Adventuresome? How did the desire for an altered state progress in your life's situations? When did it move from a desire to an absolute need? Do you believe you can live without your addiction? Why? Why not?

You may wonder why we are giving so much attention to this question. The reason is that we "use" as a symptom of other problems or needs in our lives. For this reason we have introduced this question as the first question about your adult life because it may be very important for you to see this symptom in your history in order to better understand who you were and how you felt at each stage in your personal development.

Let's face it. I don't want to try to tell you what you should or should not have done or even what you should be doing now. By itself, that won't do you any good and besides, you all ready know the answers. What we're trying to do right now is to enable you to see the relationships between your thoughts, beliefs, feelings and actions as they played out in your daily life and eventually contributed to the formation of all of your habits. Keep this in mind as you trace your steps in recording your adult life.

Introduction to Adulthood Questions and Answers

By the time we reach adulthood, the number of possible paths in which our lives may have taken is very great. We couldn't possibly construct a questionnaire that would ask you about all the possible ways in which your has life unfolded. What we can do is to select a number of key indicators that are usually found in all of our lives. You may decide that there are others necessary to capture the important aspects of how you grew up to be who you are now. Keep in mind our true objectives; we want to find out how we feel about ourselves and why. We want to find out what kinds of ideas, substances, and behaviors we have tended to abuse and to which we may have even become addicted, and why. We also want to become able to see ourselves as a family person, a friend, an employee, employer, a citizen, and even as a lover. Exactly what we do for a living makes no difference. It's not even important if we are good looking or not so good looking; all that matters is how we feel about ourselves, which may have nothing to do with how anyone else would see us. By this time in your self-examination, you almost certainly will know the why and how of all the questions about your adult reality. They flow naturally from your childhood and adolescence to such a degree that if you understand yourself up to this point, nothing about your adult life is likely to surprise you. Simply record the facts and where anything seems surprising to you; try to see how it came naturally out of your beliefs and experiences of your earlier life. It's also important that you not assume because we ask you about your sex life, your honesty, or your abuse of anything or anyone, that you are necessarily supposed to have any of these problems and challenges going on in your life. We just want to make sure if you do, that you are going to pay attention to why this is so and what role it plays in helping you or preventing you from living a happy life. By the time you get to your Fifth Gate, we will look at all of this same information from another point of view, and you will be able to achieve an even greater understanding of who you are and exactly why.

At the end of our adult questions matrix, we have included a more specific list of questions to prod you in order to help you more completely answer the questions. You may find it easier to read the specific questions at the end, before you try to fill in your matrix.

Adulthood

Take each of the following ideas and apply them one at a time to our adult subject list:

ATTITUDES, BEHAVIORS AND FEELINGS

1. I am really good at... and I feel... about this.
2. I am really bad at... and here's the way I feel about that.

3. I helped... and here's how I feel about that.

4. I hurt... and here's the way I feel about that.

5. I disappointed or made someone proud concerning... and here's the way I feel about that.

6. I harmed... and here's the way I feel about it.

7. I felt/feel ashamed about....

8. I felt/feel grateful for...

9. I felt/feel needful of... and here's how I feel about that.

10. I believe/believed I am/was addicted to... and here's how I feel about that.

11. I feel powerless over... and here's how I feel about that.

12. I feel resentful over.... and here's how I feel about that.

13. I regret... and here's how I feel about that.

14. I feel confused by... and here's how I feel about that.

15. I dread... and I think it's because...

LIFE DEPARTMENTS

1. Education

2. Athletics

3. Relationships with Family Members

4. Friendships

5. Sexual Relationships or Romances

6. Work/Career

7. Alcohol, Drugs, or other Substances

8. Lawfulness or Unlawfulness

9. Honesty or Dishonesty

10. Prosperity or Poverty

11. Hetrosexuality or Homosexuality

12. Self-Confidence

13. Marriages and Other Commitments

14. Parenthood

15. Illness or Disabilities

For each of the Attitudes, Behaviors, and Feelings listed above, you should chart or record what's true of you for each of the Life Departments. This means you could theoretically have more than a hundred entries, even though most of will have less than a few dozen that are meaningful.

When you get to the Fifth Gate, or even before then if you like, you will want to trace each of your actions, attitudes, and feelings in each Life Department in which you have had meaningful entries to try and find out how you came to think, feel, and behave that way. The answers always start somewhere in our childhood and are usually reflected by feelings and events in our adolescense. By the time we're adults, and especially once we have learned to look at ourselves as adults, we may be tempted to think of ourselves as fatalists. A fatalist is someone who believes that everything that happened was determined long before it happened. Once we take the Five Gates Training we will start to feel the power rising within us, which is our power to reshape our future based on this wonderful opportunity for self-understanding in the present. Please keep in mind that what you are now doing is so important that it is likely to positively to affect the rest of your life. Don't become impatient or short-change the process of your self-examination.

1. When, how, and in which situations did your selfish quest for sex damage other people and/or you? What people were hurt? How badly? Did you spoil your marriage and/or injure your children? Did you jeopardize your or anyone else's standing in the community? How did you react to these situations at the time? Did you feel guilty? Did you feel you were the pursued, not the pursuer, and thus absolve yourself? How have you reacted to frustration in sexual matters? When denied, did you become vengeful or depressed? Did you "take it out" on other people? If there was rejection or coldness at home, did you use this as a reason for promiscuity? Many people who are lonely and don't really

know how to love get involved senselessly in sexual escapades. Our temporary relief from loneliness makes on-call sex seem like "love." When our sex partner is gone, it makes for an even greater feeling of loneliness. Have you experienced this? If you have married a cold, unloving person, ask yourself why you chose that person to be your mate. Did you use it as an excuse to find new romances? Was your mother or father cold and unloving, and is this your chance to get even with them through your spouse? Why did you get married? Did you marry earlier than your peer group? Later? Do you resent the responsibilities of marriage and family? If married, do you allow your family to come between you and your spouse? Are you still a baby in your parents' eyes, and take advantage of this? Are you a baby in the eyes of your spouse? Have your parents gotten you out of trouble that you should have been able to handle yourself? Do you write bad checks? Do you feel that the world owes you a living? Do you gossip about others? Are laws made for other people? Do you have the right to make up your own laws as you go along? If revenge were possible right now, who would be the top people on your list? Why?

2. What are your present feelings about sex, parents, brothers, sisters, grandparents, friends, your children, your spouse, your intimate friends, your job, upon being an alcoholic or afflicted with other emotional problems? Finances? Divorce or marriage? What are your hopes and goals? Do you use sex as a punishment or reward? How much time do you spend with your family? With other recovering people? What is your greatest fear? What is your sex life like? Is it as mature as you might want it to be? Are you careless of your partner's feelings? Write out your ideal of a healthy sex life. Write out all perverted sexual experiences, such as with members of your own family, animals, etc. Do you engage in sex in order to build your own ego by conquest? Are you afraid of being sexually rejected? Are you ashamed of your body and the way you look? Write out what's wrong with you. Write out your feelings of pride about any of these questions, such as the

best things about you physically. Now write out the things about yourself that you are ashamed of. Do you use people to get what you want? Do you gossip or perform character assassinations on another in order to appear better in the business or social world? Or do you do this in an effort to feel superior, positioning yourself as the one gossiped about? If you are a thief, what have you stolen? Don't forget to include your employer's time and the good feelings others had that you might have destroyed. Do you have a pattern or getting sick? Be honest. Do you use illness as an excuse to avoid responsibilities or get attention or sympathy, to get out of a jam? In business relationships, write out your resentments toward bosses and co-workers. Do you feel jealous of them? Are you concerned that others in your office will get more money or prestige than you will? List all negative feelings you have about the people involved in your work life. Are you indifferent and careless of your job? Do you maybe think you should be the boss? Do you use the excuse that because you are recovered now, that your boss, or your family and friends shouldn't expect too much of you? If you are divorced or getting divorced, write out negative feelings about the situation and the people involved, resentments, fears, and feelings of guilt concerning your relationship with your spouse, including feelings about your children. Have you set up a game where your children are forced to make a decision about which parent they love the most?

3. If married, write out exactly how you feel about your spouse and children. Are they living up to your expectations? What are your expectations? Are they reasonable? How do you think your life would be different if they were out of your life? Do you feel that no one really understands you? Do you feel that if they only knew what you had been through, they wouldn't expect so much from you? Do you feel different or apart from others? Do you feel superior or inferior? Do you judge or make fun of people who appear to be less fortunate mentally, physically, or morally than you think you are? Do you compare yourself to others? People who are talented or

further along in areas you are not? How were you five days ago, five weeks ago, five months ago, five years ago? How are you different now? Forget how other people are (don't judge them or yourself). Work on yourself. List every act that you swore you would take to the grave, disclosing to no one. Be open and honest. Remember, life gave you good and bad experiences. Usually, the things you are the most ashamed of are the very acts that made you try to do better. Are you afraid of getting too close to another person for the fear of being rejected? Do you reject others before they can reject you? What do you feel love is? In what ways are you a responsible person? Are you a tightwad? What are your fears concerning money? Do you spend money with no thought of tomorrow? Is your personal appearance particularly careless or prideful? On sight, do you judge people by appearance? What things make you feel greedy, envious or angry? Are you scornful of ideas that aren't your own? Do you tell others how bad you have been or are? Do you consider intelligent and educated people with respect and acceptance? Do you desire to learn from them?

4. Write your feelings for parents, brothers, sisters or other family members now. What resentments do you still have? What makes you feel guilty? Do you pad your expense account or use food allowances to buy things just for yourself? Do you feel resentment toward another recovering person? What kinds of things do you lie about the most? Do you still need to play the big shot? Are you hurt when people turn away from you and won't play your games? Do you use others' weaknesses to indulge in your sexual gratification? Or does just the consideration of this make you feel guilty for having such thoughts. What kinds of things do you waste most time worrying about, the future or the past? Do you find yourself punishing your children the way your parents punished you? Have you been so busy trying to make money that your family sees little of you? Do you say, "I give my family everything they want, but they aren't ever satisfied? Are you working to build your own ego? When your spouse

turns cold, do you spend more time with him/her, or do you turn to someone else, someone you perceive has more understanding? Do you take at least one night a week for the family only? Have communications with your family members become so intolerable that you are depending on fellowship members to get your necessary strokes? Do you feel that you somehow have to prove that you are worthy of love from others, either in fellowship or elsewhere? Elaborate on this. Are you cold and indifferent to your family, friends, work or your own needs? Are you loaded with a sense of guilt for putting people through so much hell? Do you threaten others by saying that you can't resist "using" if you don't get your family back, your own way, etc. Are you involved in a love affair that could bring yourself, or others, harm? Do you argue with people? Is it important for you to be right? Do you worry about other people's Higher Power not being as good as yours, or maybe even better? Are you comparing yourself with others in spiritual growth? Do you feel superior spiritually? Do you still feel guilty about masturbation? Do you feel superior because you have more education, money, brains, the right color skin, social background, vocation, or any other seeming advantages? List all your feelings of superiority. Do you feel inferior because you have less than all of the above? List your feelings of inferiority. Do you think you are superior to the general run of people? Please list in what way(s) you are different. Do you have a hard time getting to places on time? Do you resent others who don't seem to have problems finding happiness? Are you still judging the outside of others by the inside of you? Have you bothered to ask the people who seem happy how they got that way? Do you envy people who can drink? Use drugs? Gamble? Eat what they please? Are you hostile because you don't like the hand life has dealt you? What are your present fears? How do you presently get people's attention? Pouting, sulking, temper tantrums, being extra good (and letting them know it), playing stupid, frustrating other's activities or bitching, so that others will know how bad you feel?

5. In addition to your "using" problem, what else may
    contribute to financial instability? Did fear and inferiority
    about your own fitness for your job destroy your confidence
    and fill you with conflict? Did you try to cover up those
    feelings of inadequacy by bluffing, cheating, lying or evading
    responsibility? Or by griping that others failed to recognize
    your truly exceptional abilities? Did you overvalue yourself
    and play the big shot? Did you have such unprincipled
    ambition that you double-crossed and undercut your
    associates? Were you extravagant? Did you recklessly borrow
    money, caring little whether it was repaid or not? Were you a
    cheapskate, refusing to support your family properly? Did
    you try to cut corners financially? What about quick money
    deals, the long-shot "sure thing" that would rocket you to
    riches? Businesswomen in recovery will naturally find that
    many of these questions apply to them, too. But an addicted
    housewife can also make her family financially insecure. She
    can juggle charge accounts, manipulate the food budget,
    spend her afternoons gambling, and run her husband into
    debts by being irresponsible, wasteful and extravagant. The
    most common symptoms of emotional insecurity are worry,
    anger, self-pity and depression. These stem from causes,
    which sometimes seem to be within us, and at other times
    from without. To take inventory in this respect, we ought to
    carefully consider all personal relationships that bring
    continuous and recurring trouble. It should be remembered
    that this kind of insecurity might arise in any areas where
    instincts are threatened. Looking at both past and present,
    what sex situations have caused you anxiety, bitterness,
    frustration, or depression? Appraising each situation fairly,
    can you see where you have been at fault? Did these
    perplexities beset you because of selfishness or unreasonable
    demands? Or, if your disturbance was seemingly caused by
    the behavior of others, why do you lack the ability to accept
    conditions you cannot change? These are the sorts of
    fundamental inquiries that can disclose the source of your
    discomfort and indicate whether you may be able to alter
    your own conduct and so adjust yourself serenely to self-

discipline. Suppose that financial insecurity constantly arouses these same feelings. You can ask yourself to what extent have your own mistakes fed your gnawing anxieties, and if the actions of others are part of the cause, what can you do about that. If you are unable to change the present state of affairs, are you willing to take the measures necessary to shape your life to conditions as they really are?

When you finish making your notes answering these questions, you should go onto your Fifth Gate but first give yourself a good rest since the job you just completed is both critical and highly demanding of you. You don't want to start the Fifth Gate worn out and starting the Fifth Gate with a fresh mind will trigger even more insights you may have missed in your Fourth Gate. Make sure you allow plenty of time to do your Fifth Gate in one session. You will see that it all was inevitable and not your fault. But you can change it, and improve yourself and your life by living by the principles given in the Second and Third Gates.

You must reconcile your past and the negative ideas and feelings you got from it in order to manage yourself in the present. We have already examined the idea that the present is the symptom or result of the collective past and all the things that went into our statement: "I have been powerless over something in me that has caused me to believe and therefore feel, to think and therefore do things that have diminished my happiness. That something has been my ignorance and the fears that came of my ignorance and I don't want them to run my life anymore. I wish to run my life by positive, more realistic principles – the rules of reality." These things we learn as we pass through the first three Gates, but even though we may try our absolute best to live by those positive principles, the fact is that the present is the result of our flawed past. But we can't change the past, so what are we to do? Are we truly stuck in a present from which we can never escape the ill effects of our past? That is the miracle of the Five Gates. We are not so completely stuck, nor will we ever be so completely free.

Experience has shown that there is a way to vicariously travel a path that is very similar to reliving the past, but reliving it in such as to escape the effects of mistaken ideas that we have needed in order to be right thinking in the present. This process of vicariously reliving and reconciling the past is our Fourth and Fifth Gate.

After we have completed our Fourth and Fifth Gate, we will surely want to review the first three Gates with a much greater ability to actually bring about change within ourselves as the result of the wisdom contained there. With this thought in mind, we may now embark upon the very serious task of learning about who we've been. We start out by simply recording the thoughts, beliefs, feelings and actions that formed our past, and have resulted in our present.

How Do I Know if I Have Successfully Journeyed Through the Fourth Gate?

If we are acting as our own Fifth Gate Trainer, we want to be especially thorough in our Fourth Gate, which means that we may want to work overtime in trying to make certain that we have done our best not only to answer all the questions, but also even to ask ourselves if we can jog our memory some more. If we plan to take our Fifth Gate with a certified Five Gates Trainer, our job is easier, since our Trainer will have special methods of allowing us to respond to their questions. This will help jog our memories, as we connect the dots to see how we grew up to be who we are.

In either case, our job in the Fourth Gate is to make as thorough and honest and accounting of our beliefs, feelings, thoughts and actions at each stage of our lives in the sequence in which we experienced them. The sequence is very important, because we tend to experience ourselves all at one time, with everything we know about our lives right now. But this isn't what really happened. We live those events one after the next, and we took from them what we could understand from we knew at that time, not what we know now. Take as much time with this Gate as you feel will produce more facts to feed into the engine of our Fifth Gate.

THE FIFTH GATE
Statement of the Fifth Gate:

"Once I understand my history and see my self more objectively in it, I will no longer believe that I am my history, I will know—I am my possibilities."

Celebrate That We've Made It This Far

We've done a lot of work and we have been forced to look at things we didn't enjoy. Right now our life is on the "cutting room floor" and it's finally time to do the healing job of editing what all of this means to us. If we didn't have problems, we wouldn't be here. It's time for us to see how we have always been shaped, for better or worse, by all the influences that have acted upon us. Once we see this clearly, we will know "We are not our history—*we are our possibilities*." Try to stay focused on how your mistaken beliefs about yourself and life have held you prisoner.

You can take yourself through this Fifth Gate healing, or if you prefer use the help of a friend who has themselves suffered and has achieved excellent recovery. Make sure they read all of the sections leading up to this point so they will be best able to guide you now. If your suffering has been very intense and you discover that you need professional help in completing this part of the program, go to our website (www.fivegates.com) to schedule a certified Five Gates Trainer to take you through this part of the program.

Introduction to Taking Yourself Through the Fifth Gate

We experience our lives one idea and event after another, but we experience ourselves, the result of our lives, all at one time in the present without realizing exactly how we changed gradually to be who we are today.

In this self-help presentation of the Five Gates Training Program, we expanded the Fourth Gate questions to include analysis that is normally not done until we reach the Fifth Gate. The purpose of this is to make the Fifth Gate easier for you. You may wonder why we ask you to go over what seems like the same things here in the Fifth Gate. There's one major difference. In the Fourth Gate, we reached very widely for everything that might have mattered from each period of your life—childhood, adolescence, and adulthood. Here in the Fifth Gate that's not enough; we want to try to get the events exactly in sequence the best we can so that each experience will be fresh in our minds when each next experience and feeling came up. This is how we come to understand exactly how we came to be who we are and that understanding is what sets us free.

We carry the fears and shame of our childhood self into our adulthood without knowing exactly that this is why we feel troubled now. We do not easily distinguish the different people we were at different times of our life and how we evolved through the thoughts, feelings, and events of our experiences. We are constantly struggling to convince ourselves that we are adequate to meet the challenges of our life, instead of feeling that we can take the time to understand ourselves and why we are who we are and who we have been. This is not just true of you or me, this is true of every person. Now it's time to look at ourselves the way that someone else with great wisdom would look at us and understand our story and how it shaped us to be who we are—the good, the not so good, and possibly the not so happy.

You now need to divide yourself into two people—the you, you remember as you grew up and the you, and the you now need, to be who is your counselor. That was the purpose of our Fourth Gate. It forced you to experience your story as you experienced it. Now listen to your story as your own counselor who is trying to help you see what it means.

We Begin By Understanding the Lives of Our Parents and Grandparents

If you were raised by people who were not your natural parents, answer these questions for those people who raised you and who were the most important influences in your early life. Here we will refer to whoever you decided had greatest influence upon you as you grew up by calling them your parents and their parents your grandparents.

Start with your mother's history and nature, since most of us received our personal values from our mothers and our world values from our father'.

What do you know about the lives and natures of your mothers' parents? Were there reasons that they were fearful people due to economic circumstances or possibly that they were born in a different country, or spoke a different language from the world in which your mother was raised. Was there illness or other stress factors which were operating in their lives which can help you understand them. Were they able to witness loving relationships in their lives? What was the example that life set for them concerning what life and relationships were like? Was your mother's mother nurturing to her husband? Was she nurturing towards her children? Did she feel secure? Think about what you know about your mother's life and her values as they were shaped by the world in which she lived as a young woman. Did she believe that a woman's place is in the home and that a man's place is different than a woman's place? What was she taught to believe about the kind of world she lived in and the roles of men and women and the right attitudes she should have about children? Keep in mind your mother was your grandparents child and grew up in the world her parents made for her.

Now think about what your mother was like as you knew her when you were a child and how what she was like was caused by the world in which she was raised. Don't go on until you've done your best to understand how your mother got to be who she was when you born, not who she may have become as you grew up or who she may be today. Once you have a clear vision of how your mother got to be who you have known her to be at each stage her life and yours, you have completed this part of understanding the woman who raised you as her child.Ask yourself these same questions as he grew up to be the man who raised you.

In both cases, try to see what they believed about relationships and about life. Try to see how their beliefs would have influenced you. All of us accept many of our parents beliefs, but also may have rejected and reacted to them in opposite ways. Our personalities always start out in relationship with who are parents were, what they did and didn't believe and most of all by what they showed us by what they did and didn't do. Our first goal is to try and find out why. We had no power over this part of our history.

Who Was I As A Youngster?

A lot of who we were as a youngster was a natural consequence of who are parents were at that time. Try to see how their beliefs influenced what you believed as a child. Did you think life was fun? Did you believe that life was full of opportunity for you? Did you believe the world was in some ways fair or unfair? Did you believe that people who came from your background were different than other people? If so, how were they different in your mind when you were a child? Did you believe that it was your job to be honest? Loving? Law-abiding? Generous? Kind? Or possibly, just the opposite? Think not only about what your parents said, but also about what they showed you in their actions. Were the ways in which they dressed you, encouraged you, taught you manners, or taught you the importance of education are a part of how you think about these things today? How do these attitudes explain how you have been as you were growing up?

Did your parents show you through their words and actions that men and women have positive roles in each other's lives? What did their example teach you? Can you see relationships between their values and who you were as you were a child and possible later on in your life as you grew up? Did they teach you that you were secure? That you would be happy? That you could achieve what you needed to achieve? What did they teach you about love? Was their form of love, a form of giving or controlling? How much control did you have over any of this? Stop and ask yourself if it is your fault that you started life with any of the attitudes that later contributed to your problems. Stop and ask yourself, do you need to keep believing those things now?

Try to see yourself as your parents child with no control over all these influences that came upon you because of who your parents were. Wherever this is true, stop blaming yourself for the results they may have given to your life and who you have been. Don't move on until you have seen this aspect of yourself clearly, no matter how long it takes for you to fully digest the ways you are parents child and that you had no power over who you were taught to be in your childhood and as you grew up to be who you are now. Keep in mind that your personality may be the result of having rejected their values. Even that is a way in which they caused you to be who you were as a child and who you became as you grew up.

At this point, make a list of all the things about them that became things about you when you were a child. Once you have done this, examine each one of them and see clearly that you had no power and therefore no responsibility. In other words, it's not your fault—who you were as a child growing up in your parents home. Repeat this part of your Fifth Gate as necessary for you to see all of this clearly.

Siblings and Competition

Almost all of us were taught to see life as a competitive event. It starts with our siblings and how we compete with them to get our parents favor. Stop to consider whether or not your attitudes and actions towards your brothers or sisters caused you anxiety or shame. Did you parents play each of you off against each other picking favorites and giving you each rewards that may have not been given to the other? Were you the one that got the rewards? Were you the one that felt you didn't get enough rewards in the form of affection, respect, or material things? If you were, either the one that got the rewards or didn't get the rewards, you probably thought this was about you. It's important that you now see that you almost had nothing to do with this. Your parents had a system of trying to make you and your brothers and sisters do what they wanted. They did this by rewarding each of you in accordance with how well they thought you were doing what they wanted. Stop to think about who you were in this game of rewards and denials and try your best to see that who your were was caused by the world around you and who got rewarded was caused by what your parents were trying to do to make each of you to do or be what they wanted you to do or who they wanted you to be. If you were growing up as a fearful person, you could not act secure. If you didn't agree with your parents values, you also probably didn't do some of the things they wanted you to do. Maybe they sent you mixed messages saying one thing one day and a different thing another, or possibly what they said you should was not what they were doing and you felt manipulated. That's not your fault either. Very few parents are consistent with what they say at different times, and even fewer parents are consistent with what they say being also what they do. Stop to think about their motives and see how you might have been confused and mislead. Most important, stop to understand how none of this is your fault. You were always trying your best to do what you thought was the right thing according to what you understood.

You mother may have raised you without your father or visa versa. You may have been raised by someone who is not your natural parent. The point is you must try to understand the lives of whoever raised you and the explainable circumstances that made them into who they were when you were born and who they became over the time you grew up. Try to look at this as though there lives were not about you, even though we will discover they were. We want to see the lives of those who raised us in a historical sense. We want to see them as the natural consequence of the events, beliefs, and what can know about their feelings as their personalities developed before and during our childhood. Who they became after our adolescence began will probably not matter in understanding ourselves.

Keep in mind, we don't want to judge our parents, only to understand them. We want to see that if they were cheap, ashamed, uneducated, fearful, or bad tempered, that there were circumstances in their lives that shaped them to be who they were when we were born and as we grew up to become who we are.

But we don't want to judge them but see them as who they were as clearly as we can based on the information that we have. The past is unchangeable and we are not responsible for any of it. Our goal is to see who they were and if possible how they came to be who they were so we will not be tempted to judge them only to understand them the best we can.

This section is critically important because whether we like it or not, they are the world in which we were born and in our important early years, were shaped. Once you have completed this part, you are ready to go on to looking at your history.

"Acceptance is the Answer to All My Problems Today" *(Alcoholics Anonymous)*

At this point on the journey through the Fifth Gate, we face what may at first be a contradiction. We've started out with our greatest need being our need to accept (forgive) ourselves for being who we have been through each moment in time. The truth is that we deserve and absolutely need our own forgiveness and so we may have to see one's mother as a destructive influence, in some respects, and, yet, later we will also see that we need to forgive and accept her for the same reasons we will need to forgive and accept ourselves. That reason is the facts that we are the entire product of our lives, and without any negative attention, we all do things that hurt others when all we think we are doing is trying to help ourselves. If you find yourself forgiving mother for things that hurt you when you were young, this is a good thing, but don't push it. This peace giving forgiveness and acceptance of everything and everyone will happen naturally as you see yourself through clear eyes that you were never trying to hurt anyone either; you were just trying to help yourself feel good about your own life.

Once you have to your best ability mastered your mother's personality and impact upon you, it will now be your job to heal yourself by accepting her for who she really was and possibly for whom she still is. Mothers, like us, are people.

We are always tempted to believe that everyone who does anything that greatly affects us did so with the knowledge of the effect it would have upon us, or even they could have helped themselves if they were. This is the great lie from which we need liberation. We will soon see that until we have completed this process, we have been reactors to life and not truly the authors of our lives as who we shall become. Only a small percentage of people ever become the authors of their lives or their personalities (same thing!). People are always doing the best job that they know how to do to try to make them and those they love the most secure and happy life possible, even when we can see that they have done exactly the opposite of this intention. The major engine of your freedom is your complete understanding and acceptance of yours and other people's enslavement to ideas and beliefs beyond their understanding and control. True understanding is what we mean by forgiveness. We always do it for our own sake and not for theirs. At this critical junction, we must precede no further until we have absolutely come to see our mothers and female nurturers as the inescapable products of the beliefs and events of their lives. Only those who walk this path of enlightenment (or one like it) can achieve sufficient mastery over the circumstances, which shaped them into who they are or were sufficient enough to rise above. Find it in your understanding to accept that your mother was perfect at being exactly the person her life taught her to be.

When you have achieved this, you are ready to proceed doing the exact same examination of your father's parents, your father, and any other male authorities that helped shape who you came to be as a result of your childhood. Give every bit as much care and consideration of your father and his life, as you gave to your mother, and soon will give to yourself. By this time, you know the drill, and this second time should go much easier than the first unless you had some uniquely traumatic problems that came from the influence of your father or other male authority figures.

It's My Turn

We've saved you for last because you came along later. Your parents, as they were at the time you were born, were not shaped by you, but you were shaped to a large degree by the influence of your parents. It harder to be objective about ourselves when we don't understand how our lives were started and shaped by the reality our parents presented to us. It all happened when we had no understanding whatsoever. Take the same list that you went through with your mother, then your father, and apply it to yourself. Take as long you need to find yourself as a whole person who was the result of your childhood. It is very helpful to think as us temporarily as someone else who is going through the influence of ideas and events of our early lives. Don't be surprised if you start feeling sorry for the poor fellow or gal that grew up to be you. If you have problems in your life today and you have understood this story well, you probably will feel as though what really happened to you in your life was the inescapable result of your early life influences. When you can see this, you know you are really getting somewhere. Now try to tell yourself:

"It's Not My Fault that I Grew Up to be Who I Am!"

Give up credit for all the great things about you and stop taking blame for all your personal characteristics you don't like. You never were the author of this script even though it's your life; you are the script itself, you're the story!

Ask yourself questions like:

1. Did I intend to become an anxiety-ridden, depressed, or an addicted person? When did I make that decision or did the flow of my life simply present the inescapable influences that turned me into one?

2. Did I intend to grow up being a dishonest person? An insensitive person? A cruel person? A frightened person? A criminal person? A person with my problem feelings and behavior? Then ask yourself, when did I make that decision?

You will undoubtedly begin to get an ever-deepening appreciation of the fact that you were always right in feeling that you were trapped in events and in personal characteristics and behavior you didn't like, but didn't know how to overcome.

"It's Not My Fault that I Grew Up to be Who I Am!"

Go through this process again and again until you know it's true. Deeply examine your *motives* at each phase of your life and find the you, who never wanted the problem feelings and behavior that later became who you seem to be.

That's Not Who You Really Are!

There is a you, that was always in you, that only wanted to feel secure, and avoid the pains and rejections that life at times will invariably bring upon all of us.

It's Not You. It's the Poor Soul in the Story!

Work at this for as long as it takes you to see that there are two of you. The poor soul in the story, and the you, that just always wanted to feel good and stop hurting.

You're the One Who Was Never Taught How to Win, Not the Loser at Times Life has Made You to Believe You Are

If you are still unable to believe the truth of the bold headlines above, don't go any further until you can see that they are true. Go over the story starting with your mother's childhood, again and again, as many times as it takes and as deeply as you need to consider the facts of the real causes of your personality and the events in your life. Look at what you like, and don't like, and know in your heart that until you can see the forces of cause and effect that shape you, you don't know enough about yourself yet. Use your Fourth Gate Questionnaire answers to help you get the facts right, but also where you know that your Fourth Gate answers were wrong in any respect that this is a symptom of the fact that you have been walking around with beliefs about yourself that aren't true.

Think of yourself as the person with your name, your life, your beliefs, and possibly your pre-destiny to become who you became as your childhood concluded, if it did, at sometime in your teenage years. In childhood, we almost automatically accept the opinions about us that we hear from our parents, even if we don't like them, they still reach us at a very deep level. As we begin our adolescence, we express our unwillingness to believe anybody but ourselves, which often makes us, say and do some pretty stupid things, things that even we know are wrong. We become desperate to express our growing independence. For those of us with a high degree of co-dependency, or childhood in that sense, has never ended. For those of us who are by nature rebellious to the degree that only makes sense to us at the time, and often not later, we are still in that regard still experiencing our adolescence. We achieve adulthood by becoming a more balanced version of our child self, our adolescent self, and a matured more considered more logical adult self. Most of us go up and back between all of these aspects of ourselves, even after we become adults, but our codependency becomes more selective and less of a force in shaping our beliefs and our desire to be defiant becomes more tempered by rational considerations of the results of our actions.

Find yourself, understand yourself, and start the process of predicting yourself as you begin to review your personal history through each stage of your life from earliest childhood to who you are today. If any of the answers to your Fourth Gate questionnaire are still surprising to you in the light of what you have now learned in the light of who you came to be who you are, why you feel as you do, or why you have the problems or psychological limitations that you experience today, go back over your story until there are no surprises. At any point that you find a surprise in your beliefs, feelings, thoughts, or actions—go back to finding the logical causes for them in your early life and the beliefs and actions of your parents. Do not satisfy yourself with skipping past any surprise until you have thoroughly investigated its probable logical cause so it is no longer a surprise to you. This thoroughness to go no further unless you have reconciled each of your beliefs thoughts, feelings and actions, is critical to your success of taking yourself through the journey of the Fifth Gate. By now you can see how this process is a journey which will help you discover who you were, who you are, and why you will not need to continue to be anyone who has not given you joy.

How Can I Know If I Have Successfully Journeyed Through the Fifth Gate? Finally Free!!

If you finally completed the Fifth Gate you should feel free, at last. You are not able to see yourself as a character in a play which happens to be your life, and, once you accept that your story is the inescapable result of all of the forces acting upon you at the time your story unfolded, you will know deep in your heart that none of it was your fault, and who you are today, the good, the bad, and the not so happy is also not your fault. Yet, there is still more to do because if we want to really be free, we have to give this same freedom to everyone else in our story. Mother believed the things she did, and believed the things she did, because she was at each moment in time the result of her story up to that moment in time. The same is true for dad and every other person. Think about this, not only in theory, but also actually go back over the story of that which is true. You will come to see that all of life is the result of causes and effects tied inescapably one to the other by the rules of logical understandings. As our under-standings and our information increases, our freedom increases with it. Our spiritual condition becomes better and better as we stop judging people and events and focus simply on under-standing them to the degree necessary in order for us to do our only job in life; manage ourselves the best we can in this moment in time. Our only job in life is to try our best to understand, do, and later learn from doing what we believe is the next right thing to do. We know that this is our only job, because we have no other power or wisdom by which we can manage ourselves better. We must give up the idea that we can judge that anyone should have been or should be any different than they are. Everyone is perfect and being who he or she is and always will be.

We may wish our world were different than it was or is; that's the whole idea of managing ourselves in the present. We want to choose the best decisions and actions from our real choices that will help shape our world to be what we would like it to be tomorrow. To do this, we will need tools or reality rules to help guide us along the way.

PART FOUR

BEYOND THE FIFTH GATE,
THE LIFE PRACTICE

Our Re-Journey Through the Five Gates

As we look at each of the Gates through which we have passed, we see that the Fourth and the Fifth Gate are a method of reinterpreting our experiences and the mistakes we drew from our history as we were finally able to remove blockages and inaccurate views that may have built up through old reactions from how we mistakenly processed reality. We want to keep that technique handy because life will continue to challenge our self-esteem by sending us the message that we are supposed to be able to be or do what our present experience tells us we can not be or do. We must learn the habit of continuously re-examining our feelings and testing them against the new insights we have learned from our Five Gates Core Training.

The other side of perfecting our self-management tool is to master our reality rules and positive principles until they automatically become apart of us and the central guide to how we manage our lives.

In the Fourth Gate, you may have experienced certain emotions, usually emotions of discovery, the reliving of fears, the sudden experience of insights, or feelings of disorientation, as though your life were really about someone else. This objectivity is very helpful to you now because your goal is to continue to reconcile your beliefs in order to escape old feelings and perspectives. This will free you to take new more constructive actions based on a new way of processing your experience in the present.

In our First Gate we learned that something in us, our fears and the children of our fears, had taken over the management of our lives and denied us the happiness we wanted. We also learned that this "takeover" had been so deeply implanted in us that we were powerless to resist its resulting misguidance that caused us to mismanage our lives. In our Second Gate we more clearly identified the culprit as our fears as we resolved to prevent them from blocking us from the happiness we want.

Even though when we came to the Third Gate reality rules and principles we were not yet spiritually fit enough to make them a part of us to the degree that we could rely upon them to manage our lives, we were told that we were soon would be after we experienced the emotional and spiritual awakening of our Fourth and Fifth Gate Journey.

In our Fourth and Fifth Gate Journey we created a chronicle of what we thought were the events of our lives at the time we live them, the misleading and debilitating conclusions we drew from those events, and finally we were set free from this trap by vicariously reliving our earlier journey in a whole new light.

Once we were free from the most important of our misleading core beliefs we experience a emotional awakening and were now finally spiritually fit to return to our Third Gate wisdom and put the Reality Rules and Positive Principles to work in our daily lives. The Life Practice is our personal campaign to transform ourselves permanently on an ongoing basis into ever wiser, happier, and more productive people.

The Gift of Spiritual Dissatisfaction

How badly do we want to reach our greatest personal power and pleasure in life? If we continue to improve by practicing the Five Gates Training Program, we will continue to evolve to higher and higher levels of spiritual health and strength. Likewise, if we ignore our lessons from our Five Gates Core Training, and allow ourselves to drift back into our old ways of thinking, we may lose those benefits, including our good spiritual condition, and with it our natural defenses to anxieties, depression and addiction. As I began this journey, my mentor shared with me, "Lynn, there is no standing still. Experience has taught me that I must continue to make spiritual progress or fall backward." In the course of my journey back and then onto a higher spiritual plane I learned this lesson the hard way; each time I violated one of my Third Gate principles or reality rules in an important matter, I suffered a setback. If this happens to you, don't be discouraged, simply learn the lesson taught to me by my mentor and go improving.

Healing Ourselves and Our Morality

No words can persuade a person to be "good." That can only be achieved through their seeing a more accurate and less fearful view of how life works best for them. Those who willfully commit acts that bring needless suffering upon themselves or others are not happy. Happy people are generous and loving, and therefore very powerful indeed. This relationship between positive ideas, actions and feelings works in all directions. Thus, fellowship groups are most successful for those willing to do positive things in service of themselves and others. Religions are most successful in reinforcing faith in a kind and loving world when they place their emphasis on teaching their followers in positive (loving) thoughts and actions. Self-improvement programs work best for those who get early affirmations in the form of success. Always, the person who feels successful is a positive thinking and acting person, and they have received their success for this reason. Your surest road to a successful ascension in life is to put your faith, your thoughts and your actions into positive and loving deeds. You may worry that your generosity if received ungratefully will make you a fool. Those who love are never fools, but ungratefulness is the greatest symptom of foolishness. Get into the habit of counting your blessings and accept each challenge as an invitation to do something positive.

Nonjudgementalness

A key concept that powers the Five Gates Training Program is the idea that we must not be judgmental. Many people have the wrong idea about what we mean by this. In the present, we must make judgments that support our efforts to do the next right thing. For this we use our wisdom and our good intentions to manage ourselves. But when we judge that we or someone else, or the present circumstances are different than they should be, we are making a grave error. We can't change the present or the past, and so we must accept it and work with it through managing ourselves to try to bring about situations we like better. The point is that we accept the past and therefore the present without resentment wanting only to understand them for what they are and what we can learn from them. The only judgments we will ever find constructive are those which will help us do the next right thing.

My own self-judgments nearly killed me. I ran away into alcoholism when I discovered I couldn't keep up the lie that I was better than anybody else or even as good as I thought I was supposed to be. I didn't get any real freedom until I took the Five Gates Training Program. I found that we don't know how anything or anyone is supposed to be. We may have the information we believe tells us how it is, and that's useful in making our decisions. This very simple perspective grants an immense power. It unclutters the mind to the extent we allow it to. It helps us focus on things we can actually bring, and relieves us of being preoccupied with all the things that cause our neurosis, disruptive behavior and ideas.

Acceptance

As they say in the big book of Alcoholics Anonymous, "Acceptance is the answer to all my problems today...I can find no serenity until I accept that person, place, thing, or situation as being exactly the way it is suppose to be at this moment. Nothing, absolutely nothing happens in God's world by mistake." This wonderful insight fits perfectly into the idea that we must not be judgmental if we employ the wisdom it teaches us, we will stop fighting against the unchangeable and be better able to focus our calm and deliberate efforts to manage ourselves in the present. We often speak of people we call "spiritual" in their nature. These are our friends who have mastered this idea.

Monitoring Our Feelings

Once we have successfully completed our Fifth Gate and experienced a great psychic relief based on our new insights, we will be tempted to believe our job is done. The truth is that we could have at most done half the job; how we think and how we live from now on will do the other half. If our job were done we would never again experience unproductive fears, resentments, anger, or dissatisfaction with anything we can't change. As far as we know, this is impossible for mere human beings to accomplish, but we can do an increasingly good job by using our Five Gates tools.

Our feelings, especially our negative ones, are an immediate key to open the door to spiritual self-examination. Every time we experience a negative emotion we must ask ourselves, "What is the benefit of this negative feeling? Is this a symptom of my old way of thinking allowing my fears to run my life? Will my fear or anxiety make me more or less able to act effectively?" If the answer is no, as it will usually be, our job is to find out what it is that we believe which is causing us to fear instead of just simply to analyze and act effectively. Thus we want to do more than just monitor our feelings, but also to analyze them in the cold light of deciding where our negative ones originate so that we can correct those ideas which will eventually rid us of them. The reason that this self-monitoring process will eventually reduce or eliminate our unproductive fears is that we have patterns which repeat again and again until the ideas in which they are based have been invalidated sufficiently until our new ways of thinking take control over our old fear-producing thinking habits. Some Five Gates graduates have found that keeping a journal with them and making entries of these events while their day is in progress, will give them the ammunition they need to do this job most effectively.

We Are Our Best Support System

Right after finishing our Fifth Gate, many start scratching their psychic heads wondering what comes next. We need to develop a support system for ourselves, but few of us have sufficient knowledge on how to go about engineering this key part of our lives.

We are always tempted to think of support systems as something operating outside ourselves. The truth is that the only really important support system is the one we operate inside ourselves, the one we use to accept ourselves as perfect at being an ever improving us. The secret is in the idea that we are always improving, because this is our source of hope. We see that our limitations are not our shortcomings. The truth of the matter is that we will always need to be our own therapists.

We must learn who to let into our lives and not. We must immerse ourselves into a world of affirmations. We want to live among, and to the extent possible, only deal with other positive and loving people, and not the defeatists, our negative views and habits caused us to seek out in the past. We want to live in the solutions instead of the problems. We must immerse ourselves into a life of loving service, both to ourselves and others. We must celebrate our successes and most of all our good intentions even when they do not bear out in our results. When that happens, we must calmly analyze why and accept that sometimes disappointing events are driven by factors outside of our control. The world will not always make it easy for us to be loving, but instead it may behave in ways that show that others are not. We must simply stick to the business of being loving ourselves. One of my favorite expressions is, "I can love you even if you don't give me permission." If we can learn to relate this way to everything and everyone, our successful life of loving service is assured.

Support Groups

The people with whom we live, work, or with whom we go bowling can all serve as support groups for us, allowing us to practice our new way of life. But some people have found recovery fellowships and other support groups helpful too. Examples of this are group psychotherapy, the anonymous fellowships such as A.A., N.A., E.A., and others designed for those of us who have been addicted to specific problems for which the group was formed. For those of us who have been most disabled, support groups have been a necessary stepping stone to strengthening our necessary ability and resolve to recover. If you join such a group, make sure that you never let go of the idea that you and no one else must be your primary support. You can also find online support services at www.fivegates.com.

Why Do We Want to Live a Life of Loving Service?

Weren't we raised to believe that we were supposed to get all we can? Aren't goody-goodies just suckers who seem to have an irrational need to be loved? So, why is living a life of loving service going to make us happy and well?

The first thing that we hard-headed cynics will say is "it's smart to be good to other people because they will remember this and become our friends." That's true, but that's the least of it.

Living a life of loving service does its greatest amount of good inside us. It changes us inside. We like ourselves more. And, in a very interesting way, we become more convinced that the world is a better place, if only because we're in it. Experience has proven that alcoholics who give their time and service to others stayed sober, and those who only take from life continue to get drunk.

The Five Gates View on Challenges

We will still have challenges. Even if all of our Five Gates Training Program benefits have been mastered to the point that we feel like a new person, life will continue to throw challenges at us. Some examples are economic insecurity, desires to "fix" our old friends, illness, and even old habits of ideas and addictions. Just because we know better, and have finally come to love ourselves, we still have to discipline ourselves and guide ourselves every day to work toward our improvement and freedom from our old habits. The difference is that now it will be easier to get rid of the negatives we see as standing in the way of our having a good life.

We may be especially vulnerable to those closest to us, for whom we more easily take the bait of unrealistic expectations and dysfunctional, co-dependent vulnerabilities. Don't be alarmed. Just keep living by the Five Gates positive principles, and you will be improving. Monitor your feelings, actions and words. Our words betray our lingering dysfunctional thoughts.

If you find this challenge difficult to overcome, go back and review your first Four Gates, and what you learned in your Fifth Gate about yourself and life. It will restore your spiritual high, and put all your problems into a constructive perspective. You may find it helpful to join a support group or fellowship, or if you're fortunate to know someone else walking your path, connect with them and practice your new constructive way of life, especially your new insights for lovingly and realistically managing your relationships with people. If you can, come to a Five Gates Training Center or visit us online at http://www.five-gates.com and send us your thoughts and suggestions, gratitude and challenges.

We Bring Our Happiness, Pleasure and Misery with Us Everywhere

We were taught to believe that it is our worldly successes and the opinions, favors, and honors of other people are responsible for our happiness. It isn't true. Our interactions with other people and the enjoyment of comfortable worldly situations can make it easier for us to not experience the self doubts which rob us of our happiness, but the potential for everything we can feel is always within us. Our happiness and our pleasure of feeling alive and well come from our faith that we can be and do what we need to be or do to be completely adequate to the challenges of our lives. We can accomplish this adjustment in our perspectives by taking delight in our good intentions and the actions we allow to flow freely from them into our actions. We can further solidify our self-esteem, our love for being who we are, by adjusting our expectations from life and ourselves (these are the same thing) to realistic goals for self-management and personal growth, and not on the outcomes which we must accept lie completely outside control. *Our only power in life, and therefore our only job in life, is to manage ourselves the best we can in the present.* Our positive principles and reality rules must become the guideposts of our self-management efforts and improvement.

PART FIVE

SIMPLICITY IS THE ANSWER

Simplicity is the Answer — A Meditation

Sometimes I find myself out of sorts with the business of my mind. I want things to be different than they are, but each time I focus my mind on what I think should come next all I see is another problem or troubling memories. Sometimes I don't even know what it is that is bothering me, but I don't feel good. I want to find the answer to feeling good, but I'm not sure I would know it if I found it. Maybe I already found it.

At times like these, I count my fingers and toes and see if the result I get is surprising. I check to see if I am breathing, and of course I am. I mentally scan my body one area at a time from top to bottom to see if it hurts, and if it does I check to see why and if there is anything I can do about it. If anything is hurting, and I know what it is, and I know what I can do about it, or that I can't do anything about it, I must do what I can or just accept that I can't or my mind will keep spinning around in my confusion. Confusion is my real obstacle to peace of mind and it is important that I am the creator of my own confusion.

Now it's time to remind myself that all time is now; the past is unchangeable, the future is unknowable, all I have is what I understand about my choices for this moment and how my wisdom can tell me the probable outcomes of each of my choices. I must select a choice or series of choices and wholeheartedly act on them accepting the certainty that I am doing the best I can do to help myself experience the future I want. Only the choices belong to me. The results are beyond my power to control.

If I need more assurance I can take some satisfaction in knowing that logically by the rules of reality I am doing the best I can do, and once I've checked my choices and estimated their outcomes, and acted upon them that must be enough for me. My rational way of seeing things this way will be attacked by old foolish beliefs. A part of me will want to say to me that I must know, or I am supposed to be able to know the outcomes of my choices. I must dismiss this lie. It's part of how I was mistaught to see the rules of reality earlier in my life. All judgment I have is good as long as I am only judging the probable outcomes of my actions, never the value or worth of another person. My best judgment is perfect, because I am perfect at being me. People are perfect because they are perfect at being themselves, even though a part of me wants to tell me, that I know better who they should be, and therefore what they should believe and do. When I feel the tug of these wrong ideas, I must learn to laugh at myself, and pray for the day that our children will not be enslaved by the wrong beliefs that have held me a prisoner from my happiness. I demand to be free now and so I must give myself freedom from wrong thinking. I must accept that absolutely everything is exactly the way it is supposed to be for now. It does me no good to think otherwise since the past is unchangeable and the present is the inevitable perfect result of all the forces that acted in the past. My only power is in my opportunity to choose what I believe is the next right thing for me to do to make things turn out the way I would like them to be. My other power and responsibility is to accept these peace granting ideas so that I can enjoy and therefore function at my best in the present. If this hasn't worked for you yet, then you must go to the beginning of this exercise and repeat it again and again until it does. You can do it!

PART SIX

APPENDICES

Using the Five Gates Web Site

Our website at "http://www.fivegates.com" is intended to provide help for those who wish to take the Five Gates Training Program, and for those who have journeyed through the Five Gates and wish to learn from others and share their experience in this new way of life. Five Gates Certified Trainers, and recommended tapes, pamphlets, books, online seminars and therapy groups are all consistent with the Five Gates Training Program.

When Do We Need A Certified Five Gates Trainer?

Although it is recommended for the severely troubled or late-stage addicts to go to a Five Gates Training Center in order to work this program, for those less afflicted or ill, and for those who are adventurous, careful and somewhat alert, it is possible to take yourself through this program by carefully following the directions in this book. There is a patent pending on this process, and therefore it would be a violation for someone to take anyone else through this program unless he or she was a certified Five Gates Trainer. The reason for that is that I do not wish to have amateurs working with individuals at this level, and possibly bringing about harm to those who are severely troubled and highly vulnerable. This is a very serious process and must be done with great care.

For those who are taking this program on their own and acting as their own facilitator, you may be as early in the process as your first few days, or you may be a few weeks into a careful and patient self-exploration. Either way, you will want to do certain things to make it most probable that your Fifth Gate journey and reconciliation of the effects of your personal history will be successful and pleasurable.

How to Become a Certified Five Gates Trainer

Qualifications:

In my experience in taking people through the Five Gates Training Program I have found the following to be the most important elements for my own preparation to do this important job:

1. A very strong desire to help people to a degree that is selfless when you are working a particular person who needs your help.

2. You must be a Five Gates Training Graduate yourself so that you have experienced this healing process and can draw from those parts which were most valuable to you.

3. A capacity for intimacy which can only come from being healed yourself to a point that you will not use lies to try and make a point to your client.

4. Having suffered a debilitation which has forced you to accept a personal humility and acceptance of your own limitations.

5. A high degree of intelligence and energetic creativity.

6. Sufficient life experience that you can relate to people who have traveled many different paths.

If you possess these qualities, I encourage you to contact us through our website at www.fivegates.com for the purpose of learning and practicing the techniques which will enable you to become a Certified Five Gates Trainer. You should expect that your training will consist of taking the Five Gates Training Program, observing and analyzing with other interns, a Certified Trainers application of our methodologies and taking several clients through the training on your own supervised by a Certified Five Gates Trainer at our facility. In all, the process will require one to two months of full-time study and practice. Our desire is to develop as many Five Gates Certified Trainers as possible.

Statements of the Five Gates

The First Gate:

"I have been powerless over something in me that causes me to believe, and therefore feel, to think and therefore act in ways that diminish my happiness."

The Second Gate:

"That 'something' is my incorrect beliefs and the fears they bring upon me. I don't want to allow them to run my life anymore."

The Third Gate:

"I want to learn, accept, and practice living by the positive principles that work best in MY reality as it really is, not the negative ones inspired by my fears."

The Fourth Gate:

"My present is the result of my past. To understand it and myself best, I must carefully review what I can remember of my history."

The Fifth Gate:

"Once I understand my history and see my self more objectively in it, I will no longer believe that I am my history, I will know I am my possibilities."

Author's Epilogue

Expert's tell us that there are 22 million substance addicted Americans. 10% are clinically depressed and only a small percentage of us are free of anxieties, obsessive thoughts and compulsive behavior. At first these appear to be separate but overlapping problems, but in my practice I found that they are all attributable to only two causes; the way we have been taught to think and our inherited or acquired tendencies to suffer neurochemically. For along time it has been believed that our neurochemistry is a primarily independent source for these problems. My experience has convinced me that most neurochemistry problems are a result of long term and acute psychological patterns driven by our dysfunctional core beliefs which we acquire usually in childhood. In a sense I have come to believe in a unified field theory of emotional disorder which links the relationships between the dysfunctional beliefs we were taught in childhood, their resulting emotional stresses, and for many of us disabling neurochemical imbalances. The best part of this unified perspective, is that it teaches us both in theory and in my practice that most of our disabling emotional and mental problems are to a major extent reversible.

When we apply these insights to the challenge of solving most of our social and mental health problems today, we see both a mandate for changing our mental health system and a much more promising hope for our future both as individuals and as a society. It is my greatest wish that this contribution, Five Gates, The Science of Healing the Spirit will serve all of us achieve personal wellness and the mending of our suffering.

As you and others help me discover more, I will share these new insights and methods at our Five Gates website www.fivegates.com. You will find fellowship and continued support there.

About Lynn Kesselman

Born June 18, 1939 in Philadelphia, Pennsylvania, Lynn Kesselman grew up in an upper middle class Jewish community in Cherry Hill, New Jersey. His father, Louis Kesselman, was a factory worker, union organizer, and socialist. His mother, Sadie Kesselman, was the daughter of wealthy European leather industry entrepreneurs. Lynn attended public schools where he always under performed scholastically due to his undiagnosed handwriting disability (dysgraphia). Boys were not yet taught to type and laptop computers or PC's had not yet been invented. Beginning in the 4th grade he turned his full attention to mathematics and music where he showed prodigious talent. He always suffered from the feeling that he was raised among children from a higher social and economic class.

In 1957 Lynn graduated from Merchantville High School and entered Rutger's University in New Brunswick, New Jersey, where he was recognized for his exceptional mathematical talent. Under a special arrangement he was permitted to take all of his undergraduate major requirements and some graduate mathematics courses in his first year, all of which he completed successfully. At Rutger's, Lynn was a political activist campaigning against compulsory military education against which he led a successful boycott. Because of his refusal to attend ROTC and his constant cutting of classes, he was failed in ROTC, gym, and second semester honors English and was dropped.

Lynn went to work in a factory to raise money for his second semester and do to a flaw in the registration procedure was enable to re-enter Rutger's for his sophomore semester where despite his nearly perfect GPA in that semester, he was dropped. He then decided that he had had enough of the formal education system.

For the following two years he used his abilities in poker and bridge to earn a living in Philadelphia and having found this to be a dead end he relocated to Venice Beach, California in 1960, where he got a job as a support mathematician for a nuclear physics aerospace research group at Douglas Aircraft despite his lack of a degree. In 1960 he produced a research paper for NASA;

"Integrating the Boltzman's Transport Equation by Monte Carlo Computer Simulation," and thus established himself as a professional mathematician. He was awarded a full college scholarship with the right to attend classes at UCLA on company time but declined to return to school. In 1963 he produced an original research work in thermodynamics, "Demonstration of the Infeasibility of Reactor-Powered Rocketry in Space," but discovered that government research contractors were so political that Douglas Aircraft choose to ignore this discovery and continued to earn cost plus 20% on the balance of their contract. In 1964 Lynn resigned from Douglas Aircraft and all further research in natural science until his much later interest in mental health many years later.

In 1965 Lynn relocated to New Jersey where he became, after lying on his application that he had a master's degree in mathematics, Director of Scientific Inventory Management for RCA's Parts and Accessories Division. Lynn spent the next seven years applying his mathematics and computer technology knowledge to applications in the business and agricultural research sectors. In 1967 he founded Compumedia, Inc., which was very successful and by age twenty-nine Lynn was a multimillionaire. Lynn tried to expand Compumedia into a national computer service and development organization but failed due to under capitalization. 1971 he semi-retired to New York City where he took a part time principal consultant position with Artronic Information Systems, an information sciences and research brain trust, while spending most of his time enjoying the fast-paced social life of the city.

In 1976, Lynn Kesselman reincorporated Compumedia of New York as a management consulting company, which he operated successfully for two years after which he relocated to Dallas, Texas in response to outstanding real estate opportunities there. In 1978, he founded Appletree Construction Company, a real estate investment and redevelopment firm which he was forced to close down when the prime rate went to 21% in 1981 and he was tied up in a contested divorce. In 1981 Lynn relocated back to New York City where he purchased a fashion accessory manufacturing company Marvela Tanenbaum Designs and two loft buildings in Tribeca.

In 1985 Lynn married a prominent psychiatrist with whom he attended 1,500+ classroom hours of American Psychiatric CME education over the following fourteen years (1985-1998). In 1987 he began his studies in Torah/Talmud, the New Testament, and other spiritual scriptures. Despite all of his mental health, sciences, and spiritual studies, Lynn became afflicted with progressively intense anxiety problems starting in 1990 due to his marital and business difficulties. Beginning in 1990-93 he abused and progressively became dependant on alcohol as a self-medication for his anxieties. In the summer of 1993 to July 15, 1995 he suffered from eventually debilitating hard-core alcoholism.

On July 15 of 1995, in utter despair and ruin, he put a gun in his mouth but declined to go through with ending his life. This is where his journey towards self-healing and eventually healing others began. First he used and eventually developed a new understanding of the 12-step recovery program of A.A. As he continued to improve the 12-step recovery program he eventually developed his own recovery program, The Five Gates.

Lynn was very confused by the 12-step recovery program feeling that it was superstitious, judgmental, incomplete, unchanging with the times and in practice did not work for many people which he desired to help. In 1997 he completed his first book "Recover With Me," regarded by many to be a classic reinterpretation and presentation of the 12-step recovery program. Beginning in 1997, as he took many people through the 12 steps of A.A.'s program, he began to see why the program was helpful to some people but unfortunately not to most of which 90% relapsed. He also saw that too many of the remaining to stay sober were living unhappy, under productive lives. From these efforts he began his development of a new program, the Five Gates, which to our knowledge is the fastest and most powerful recovery program for emotional, and as it's practice has revealed, most mental disorders. Today in his practice he boasts an 80+% recovery rate and has written this book, "The Five Gates; The Science of Healing the Spirit," for the purpose of sharing his discoveries with the world.

Just For Fun - "Lynnisms"

My limitations are not my shortcomings. • Nothing I can't do can possibly be my job. • What I think, say and do is about me—what you say, what you think and what you do is about you, even if you say it's about me. • Everything is, was, and always be exactly as it is supposed to be. • My recovering has not failed yet just because it has not succeeded yet. • I never know how good my recovery is until it's not good enough. • I have the power to love you or like you no matter what you do or think about me. • I will always try to love everyone for my sake, not theirs. • The world is a mirror of me. • I am connected to everything and everyone and they are connected to me. • I have no idea if you're supposed to drink or use other drugs or behave in other ways. I only know it's my wish and my intention to help you be happy without needing to fall back on any compulsive behavior, and that you will have the truest maximum degree of personal power of choice and clarity that I can help you achieve. What you believe about use of this new power is entirely up to you. • People who feel empowered do not intentionally bring suffering upon others but instead tend to be loving and generous. • The greatest gift I can give you is to help you experience being who you most love to be. • Our bottom is always exactly in the place where we believe that continuing to use is immediately more painful to us than the hoped for relief of stopping. It's never based upon what I think will happen later. It's never based on what is the morally right thing to do. If I cared about that, I wouldn't have fallen into the pit of spiritual bankruptcy.

We all have some faith in something or we would be driven mad by our fears. We intuitively believe the sun will rise in the morning and the laws of gravity will continue to operate upon us so we won't fly off this planet. But do we believe that we can have a secure and pleasurable life? It is the restoration of that faith that is our real recovery. Once we have that, the steps to wellness are easy to take.

I am not my history, I am my possibilities!!

Five Gates Audio Presentations by Lynn Kesselman

To listen to audio presentations of key insights from the Five Gates program go to www.fivegates.com where you will find downloadable lectures on each point priced separately.

Members who sign up at www.fivegates.com will receive free coupons to listen to Lynn's lectures. Topics are on the following page.

Why do I do things I know are no good for me?
What is recovery?
How do you know if you need to be in recovery?
Explanation of the 12-step recovery program (3 parts)
How did I become who I am?
How can I become happy?
The Five Gates approach to personality change and healing
Family members and recovery (2 parts)
The role of faith in recovery
Romance and recovery
What can I do if my life is tied to an addict?
What can I do if my life is tied to a depressed person?
About rage and violence (2 parts)?
Do I need AA or a fellowship?
What is it like to go to AA?
Selecting a therapist
Can I heal myself? (2 parts)
How long does it take to recover?
Is my emotional or mental disorder physical?
Should I drink ever again?
What makes me keep using?
Is recovery time important?
How can I speed up my recovery?
How can I get help from my love one?
What is my self-esteem and what can I do about it?
Is smoking cigarettes different?
Should family members go into recovery together?
I'm fine, but I want more? Why?
Understanding relapses
What is obsessive compulsive disorder?
What is bipolarity?
What about Treatment Centers and Halfway Houses?
Why do I need so much?
Why am I obsessed by old baggage?
What is spirituality?
What about religion?
Did my problems start in childhood?
How can I take therapy sessions with Lynn Kesselman online?

Continue Your Journey of the Five Gates Training Program with Us

Many graduates of The Five Gates Training Program have found added enlightenment and considerable enjoyment in sharing their ideas and experience with other Five Gates graduates. To join with us, please visit our website at www.fivegates.com.

Additional Five Gates Materials:

Recover With Me

Lynn Kesselman's classic presentation of the 12-step recovery program from a Five Gates perspective.

Free to Love My Life

The Five Gates program presented so you can take yourself through the Five Gates program from audio tapes or CDs

Five Gates Audio Presentations by Lynn Kesselman

To listen to audio presentations of key insights from the Five Gates program where you will find downloadable lectures on each point priced separately. Members who sign up at www.fivegates.com will receive free coupons to listen to Lynn's lectures. Topics can be found on the preceding page.